SONG IN HIGH SUMMER

by

Paul Baker

SOURCE BOOKS/ECHOES OF SILENCE
Trabuco Canyon CA 92678

Produced in the USA by Source Books/Echoes of Silence.

The publishers thank the LA Weekly, Los Angeles, for permission to reproduce their article *Women As Targets;* Joan Jara for permission to quote from her book *Victor, An Unfinished Song;* and Orbis Books for permission to take a passage from *Blood of the Innocent* by Teofilo Cabastrero.

ISBN 0 940147 06 8

Source Books   P.O. Box 794   Trabuco Canyon   CA 92678

Printed in the U.S.A. by KNI, Inc., Anaheim, CA

Dedicated with grateful love
to my one family of many families:
Chilean, English, Salvadoran,
Scottish, Nicaraguan, North
American. And especially to all
the women of that family.

Chile: 26th May 1989

Dear Paul,

I was very moved by your book...I found many
parallels between you and Victor. I can really imagine
you two passing the guitar from one to the other,
discussing, telling anecdotes and even drinking endless
cups of tea—also Victor's favourite beverage.
Perhaps one day we shall meet. I hope so. Meanwhile,
my best wishes for your book.

Un abrazo,
Joan

Foreword

Paul Baker has written a moving and dramatic testimony
of love and solidarity confronting persecution, terror and
torture. As a living witness he has managed, for an instant,
to draw the curtain which conceals so much unwritten
human history, showing the day-by-day courage of those
who struggle, against enormous odds, for social justice and
the basic necessities of life, whether in El Salvador, Chile,
South Africa or the slums of Glasgow.

His book is also a testimony of the role that music and
song can play in that struggle as a means of solace, of
integration and communication across language and
cultural barriers. Victor Jara was killed in Chile in 1973
because of his songs; now, many years later, Paul Baker, a
man from a very different country, keeps those songs alive
by singing them in a context which is the continuation of
that same struggle for social justice, peace and freedom
from exploitation for which Victor gave his life. I wish that
history could have allowed them to meet. They would have
been friends.

Joan Jara

Contents

Foreword

You Ask Us Why We Sing   1

Journal at the Frontline 1   2
1   The Songs of Solitude   5
    Journal at the Frontline 2   18
2   Echoes of the Weeping Rain   27
    Journal at the Frontline 3   40
3   For Those Who Died Screaming   45
    Journal at the Frontline 4   60
4   For Those Who Laugh in the Darkness   67
    Journal at the Frontline 5   85
5   For Those Who Die Singing   96
    Journal at the Frontline 6   115
6   Ay Nicaragua, Nicaraguita   119
    Journal at the Frontline 7   145
7   My Own Revenge: Mi Venganza Personal   153

    ¡Canta, Mi Pueblo, Canta!:
    Sing, Oh Sing, My People!   178

YOU ASK US WHY WE SING . . .

We sing for those who died in the silence
For those who died weeping
For those who died screaming
For those who died quietly
From hunger and lack of clean water

We sing for those who dream, stubbornly, for justice
For those who laugh in the darkness
For those who die singing
For those who work
Endlessly labour
For life, for freedom

For we know that greed and despair
Poverty and torture and war
Are not our true selves
That love and gentle resolve
Our song and our silence
Are stronger than death
And that,
At the end,
They will not falter

(Chilean song: Anonymous)

Journal at the Frontline 1

I thought I had this book under control: the song of my life in full summer. But it's blown up in my face.

The death squads used a stick to rape Yanira. Front and back —again and again. They cut her tongue and her hands; they burned her with cigarettes. They kicked her in the stomach. They beat her over and over, on the head, in the face. They tore the initials E and M into the palms of her hands. They started to skin her. After six hours, they threw her, naked, out of the van, down the side of a freeway overpass.

E and M stand for "Escuadrones de la Muerte": Death squads.

The policeman who found her just left her: walked away; dazed and horribly wounded, she couldn't answer to his satisfaction.

Even now she's still ripped to pieces inside. It's almost certain that she'll never be able to have a child again. She suffers massive headaches and recurring pain; her eyesight is distorted; and her little son, 3 1/2 when she was attacked, is traumatised.

She was just 22.

Guatemala? El Salvador?
No. Los Angeles, California.

Why?
Us.

Our coffee: our consumerist society: our greed, institutionalised. Coffee (and other 'cash crops') are grown *in El Salvador on the lands taken from the dispossessed. Yanira is part of her people's movement for justice, for food, for life. They claim that land back from the oligarchy and their paymasters, the international companies, ourselves. So they are attacked. Our coffee, their blood.*

I was just passing through, on my way home to Scotland. I'm a musician and singer. I'd been in Washington D.C. representing Scottish people who'd travelled to Latin America in a huge demonstration against the war there, which brought 80,000 people into Mr. Reagan's capital in April 1987.
The songs I sing are largely echoes of that war: from Chile, from Nicaragua. Now, especially, from El Salvador.

After Washington I set out to meet as many musicians and fellow workers as I could. By now I should have been well back in Edinburgh, settling into a quiet rhythm to get this book written.

Instead I find myself crouched in a pizza house in downtown LA. The musack is roaring loud, people hustling by. I have just one hour before picking Yani up. Carlos is with her. The latest threats have sworn to pull his head off—because she will not stop her work for justice.

This is going to have to be the pattern: a few sentences snatched out of borrowed time and flung onto the page. Little studious sifting and balancing. Part book, part war dispatch.

It'll be better like this. It's being written at white heat: to try to let people taste what's going on. To bring home this war—war—being waged against the ordinary people of the earth. A war—waged by our democracies, which claim to be developed—which first robs them of their inheritance, and then brands them subversives, terrorists when they dare to try to take that inheritance back. Even though to reclaim the right of their children to decent food and education and homes is all their goal. As Woody Guthrie would say:

"As through this world I ramble I seen lots of robber men:
Some rob you with a sixgun: some with a fountain pen"

To make us angry—angry enough to commit ourselves to stopping the mayhem which our governments: the US and the other countries of the rich North—Britain foremost—have been allowed to visit on the impoverished ones of the earth.

It's written to help give voice to the children and the women and the men whose voices are suppressed by those who stalk the corridors of greedy power. To listen to those voices—especially as so often, against all the odds, they speak of beauty, gentle, passionate resolve and powerful love, inseparably from anger and right and revolution.
Because of this beauty, it's part poem too: the verses integral to the text. The whole thing should really be sung.

So let it be, then, the song of all the Yaniras of the world, in their high summer of glowing courage and tender resoluteness, their laughter and inextinguishable life.

And of my gratitude for being asked to sing along.

1 The Songs of Solitude

"Empieza el llanto de la guitarra . . . es inutil callarla . . .
es imposible callarla . . . "

"The cry of the guitar begins
The winecups of daybreak are broken
The cry of the guitar begins.

It is useless to hush it
It is impossible to hush it
It weeps unending as the water weeps
as the wind weeps
over the snowfall
It is impossible to hush it

It weeps for things far away
sand of the warm South
asking for the white camelias
It weeps
arrow without target
evening without morning
and the first dead bird upon the branch

Oh, guitar!
Heart grievously wounded by five swords."

(La guitarra: Federico Garcia Lorca)

The guitar and song are in my blood: who knows why, or where they came from. What matters is the music itself, the guitar which gave it birth—and all the friends, shared life and courage that they have given me.

The road to the pizza house began with the guitar. And with its birth in fierce revolution within a monastery of strict silence.

I don't know why I tried to become a hermit. I was 21. I'd just managed to overcome a paralysing awe of women which had kept me admiring them, at a distance, throughout my teens. So I was deep in a torrid love affair with Cathy. I was already playing music: jazz trumpet, not well but passionately. Vitally I was listening, listening with all my heart: to the great blues singers and eternally to Beethoven quartets and Bach and Bartok and Mozart.

Perhaps it was the echoes of the silence which all great music, all truly passionate communication, must be rooted in which caught my inward ear: sounding deeper than any note and more profoundly still than any tree, tremulous, and waiting on the storm.

The only thing I know is that it's to the still heart of the music, and to the tender heartland of love's silences that I have to turn in trying to speak about this time. Fascinating that the hermit's life—the way of aloneness—should ring so true to our closest communion as human beings: not just the words of love, but the gestures, the movements of the hands, the glances, the special silences, the sudden smiles, radiant with long intimacy. And wonderful that, for all its horror, Yanira's story speaks those same silences.

In the whole of the British Isles, with their 60,000,000 people, there were just 60 hermit monks in 1961. The training was fierce—not so much in terms of the rigours of the monastic way itself—much more in the searing demands of solitude. Most of us were not able for it: no matter that we liked to spend time alone, no matter that we believed absolutely in our God of love and so had gone apart to be with him.

The first three months were wonderful: a sweetly lovely spring cascading into my tiny cell each morning with the lifting sun. A myriad little birds, diving and spiralling through the densely jungled garden. The silent steeple of the main church, standing serene in the circle of cells, uniting our separateness in the one single goal of worship.

As novices, beginners in the art of silence, we were not left entirely alone. To begin, Fr. Joseph, the senior monk dedicated to our guidance, came by once each day. Then less frequently: every other day; every week.

Time passed like smoke: praying eight times through the 24 hours: hours of meditative reading: study: food twice, once around midday, once towards evening: sweet sessions in my own garden.

Suddenly the light went out.

The days were as fine: the birds sang as truly.

But the thread was cut through. The sun turned searchlight, probing to the deepest nerve; the silence became the white wall of God's anger, deafening in its blankness; the cell became a prison indeed, for all that its door was still unlocked.

I was there, alone, for *ever*. Alone in the beauty, yes, but alone also in the searing loneliness. Forever—and by my own hand.

In the end I too was not capable of enduring the solitude. I belonged with the 60,000,000 and not with the select 60.

The world fell to pieces. Gouging shards of guilt which tore me apart. I stood condemned as a renegade, rejecting God's call.

I begged to be taken back.

The Charterhouse—built like a prison, with all its windows facing inwards—was impregnable to every frantic effort. Fr. Joseph was implacably against my tearing the walls back down. All my pieties, once so natural, were suddenly the formulae of madness, jangling to lunacy in the gulf fixed between us.

There was no going back.

The family, loving as always, took me in without question. They gave me room, held my hand, even delivered the occasional kick to get me out of myself. In these early sixties, there were plenty of jobs about. I worked for a gloomy while in the bowels of Burns and Oates, by Westminster Cathedral in London—selling candlesticks and altar breads. The place did little for my shattered peace, with its ecclesiastical clutter of fear and tearing guilt.

A friend, Gordon, asked me to work at his timber yard. There, with immense relief, I found fresh air working outdoors, more money, companionship, and a love of wood which would blossom in its own time into the monastery-built guitar.

Fr. Joseph's last words had been: "Find some priest as spiritual guide."

All the local priests were too busy. More used to 'problem' people just pitching up the cathedral ran a round-the-clock service of counsellors. There, at last, I heard someone say: "Come see me every week." Fr. Adrian Arrowsmith.

Six months later, I was on my way to Nunraw: "the Nuns' House." Near Edinburgh, Nunraw was being recolonised for the contemplative monastic life some three or four hundred years after the last of its nuns had been sent packing by the Reformation. The newcomers were Cistercian monks rather than nuns. They had come, in 1942, from Ireland, where the flame flickered on, to revive the phoenix.

I went because I was told to. My heart was still set on the

Carthusians. But it was a relief to have someone else take the decisions.

Nunraw wasn't as isolated as I'd hoped. A public road ran right through its land. It wasn't very much used though, and we were way out in the country folded into the foothills of the Lammermuirs. The monks' seculsion was maintained by the size of their holding. They had 1,300 acres which began with barley, wheat and oats, and ended against the skyline and among the heather with the hill sheep. Beef cattle between; a dairy and a large garden. Where the Carthusians had focused their search for God around actual physical solitude, the core of Cisterian life was community. *Everything* was done together: we ate together, read together, prayed together, studied together, worked side by side in the fields. We even slept together, modesty strictly preserved by a screen between each bed. Each monk set out his small personal pool of quiet by adhering sternly to the rule of silence for which the order was celebrated. As with the Carthusians, the novices could speak to the Novice Master, if such speech was absolutely necessary. The officers of the monastery spoke to one another, as sparely as possible. And the Abbot, spiritual father to the whole community, could speak as he judged appropriate. That was it.

Somehow I put up a good enough showing to be offered a novice's place, and I went home to torch the bridges all over again. The family stood quiet, bravely watching the small glimmers of strength they'd given me being sucked back into the storm. No-one could really make any sense of it. For all that my mother and we five children were cradle-Catholics, the contemplative life was thought to be too rarefied for us to understand. The poison of functionalism: "Do something *useful*, for heaven's sake!" had corroded the intangible down to the incomprehensible. The monks simply farmed the land, and read and prayed. They had no "worth"; they did nothing externally useful. No school; no parish; no hospital; no preaching mission. They farmed to keep themselves alive, housed and praying. Take or leave it.

My father had, from his late teens, found major tenets of his own family's brand of Christianity: the Methodism of Charles Wesley, increasingly hard to accept, and had long been agnostic. Later, his passion for my lovely mother drove him to examine Catholicism, but the explanations of the priests only confirmed him in his position. None of the churches made sense: the gap between their preaching and practice was too wide.

Yet I think he had a deeper grasp of what the monastic life was about than the rest of us—maybe his lifelong love of growing things helped. But he saw it clearly—*and* my limitations. "I give him 6 months," he'd said, driving away his carfull of weeping family from the hermitage gates.

I lasted 4 1/2.

Father wrote later saying how his heart had dropped as I set out again for the monastery. He had hoped that first bite would have rendered me everlastingly shy.

But each of us was different; some seemed to need religion, although for him it was just one more way for we confused human beings to try to make some sense of an essentially random universe. "Just because we're always looking for a meaning doesn't mean that there is one," I can still hear him saying, as we tried to fit the pattern of God's love to the dreadful death, by cancer, of one of our uncles.

That remark stuck like a burr. And, for me, his faithful humaneness now echoes in the music "born in blood" of Victor Jara and the rest:

"La luna siempre es muy linda, y el sol muere cada tarde. . .
Playing at angels and at devils: playing at the child
who will never be born:
The candles always burning:
we have to seek refuge in "Heaven."
Where are we to get the money

to pay for faith?
All I know is the moon is always beautiful,
and the sun sets each night.
I want to cry out: 'I believe in nothing other besides the
warmth of your hand, close here in mine.'"

**(La Luna siempre es muy Linda: The Moon is always
beautiful: Victor Jara)**

Victor, the great Chilean poet and singer, was murdered
for daring to challenge the effects of the supposedly
Christian civilisation imposed on his people by the
depradations of the multinationals. His words seem ever
more closely to fit reality. For I now know at first hand how
Christian presidents and Christian Democrats actively back
torturers and death squads, refusing to listen to those who
suffer at their hands. Protestants and Catholics blow each
other's little children to pieces. Buying turkeys and
expensive trash is more important to Christians at Christmas than caring for those who have no homes.
    And my own sister is mutilated for daring to dream,
simply, of every child with food, and every family with a
home, and all of us "Free at last."

The monastery was a large country house, bought over
from a family named Cockburn. The founding monks had
begun a further building designed to accommodate 100.
This optimism seemed well justified, for when I arrived the
community was already more than 60, just 20 years after its
beginning.
    December 1962. The omens were not good. The
morning of my induction, dark and cracking with cold, the
electricity supply collapsed. To me this was one more sign
of divine anger. It was all I could do not to run screaming
into the blackness. Not about to have any such nonsense,

the novice master, Fr. Andrew, hustled me down dark corridors, more by touch than sight, until we suddenly spilled out into the church. Candles had been pressed calmly into service, and the principal work of the monks, their 'Divine Office,' went quietly and dauntlessly on.

This was the office of the first hour. As it ended I was swept up into the eddying cowls and whirled off to the Chapter House. Here the hapless newcomer had to prostrate himself before the community, ritually asking for admission.

At that time there were three novices with a simple promise to stay for up to two years. After the two years their white tabard would be exchanged for a black one, their promise for three vows: poverty, chastity and obedience, they would begin their studies for the priesthood. Again three years and the all-enveloping cowl would replace their cloaks, symbolising their permanent immersion in the monastic way.

Watching the monks file out of chapter, hoods up, hands enfolded in cowl sleeves, eyes down, there was no hint of the maelstrom which was to all but wreck the monastery in the time just ahead. The Second Vatican Council and I arrived pretty much together. It ushered in the most turbulent ten years in the Catholic church since the Reformation itself. Sixty-six monks when I joined, the community would be down to 35 the day I left in 1970. Ten years later there would be only 25.

The first few weeks at Nunraw were spent learning the seemingly unchangeable rules of the life. The Cistercians had been in existence since 1098, when they broke away from the Benedictines (founded in the 5th century). They were in search of a more complete observance of 'The Rule.' This short document had been written by Benedict of Monte Cassino, in Italy, and it had quickly spread throughout Christendom.

The Cistercians were themselves reformed in the 17th Century. The abbot of La Trappe, in northern France, the Abbé de Rancé, tightened up on the observance of silence, the strictness of diet, and other areas where laxity had become common. His reform swept the order like wildfire. The Cistercians are better known as Trappists to this day.

By the 1960s the reform had decayed into dreary legalism, without the flexibility needed to ride out the coming storm.

Obedience had become the primary focus of the life: the good religious was the obedient religious above all. Contemplation—the craft of being still, with God, was effectively secondary.

Where St. Benedict's Rule was vague and poetic, the Trappists had developed 'Regulations,' detailed and unrelentingly prosaic: "When drinking, the cup must be held by *both* handles"; "Monks always walk in single file, with the hems of their robes tucked up, their arms folded."

For me, obsessed with the minutiae of supposed guilt, they were a minefield.

In those days the monastic way still seemed immutable.

Yet when the cataclysm struck many of us found that the substance of the life had corroded away beneath the rigid formulae, and there was no strength left.

The monks were good for me. Apart from Fr. Andrew's constant dismissal of the phantoms of despair, the company and the outdoor work brought me back to some sanity. In those times before agribusiness crushed out so much of the gentleness of the life, we novices formed a rent-a-gang work force. We hoed turnips and stacked hay and carted manure and fixed fences. Sometimes the sun shone, usually the winds blew, every winter the snow piled high.

My curls were shorn away. I was dressed in new clothes

and given a new name, Paul. All this to symbolise rebirth in God.

And I finally took full part in the rhythms of the day. Both monasteries followed the traditional Christian practice of praying through the darkest parts of the night. The Carthusians, extreme as ever, went to bed each evening at 6:30. Four hours later they dragged themselves from their deepest sleep to spend the next three praying in the tomblike cold of the church. Then back to bed, frozen, tugging the ragged edges of sleep around them, numbly dreading the morning bell, ticking down to 6:30. The Trappists, for all their rigour, had ruled out getting up twice every day: they were in bed by 7:30 in the evening, and up again at 2:00 am. Six-and-a-half hours sleep isn't that much, especially after a long day in the fields, but it *was* uninterrupted and, after the Carthusians, seemed almost indulgent.

At last I found myself beginning to look forward to each day with some conjuring of eagerness.

I took my 3 year vows in 1965. Just in time. John XXIII, the 'caretaker' pope, an old man put in to hold the conservative line, suddenly blew the lid off the old comfortable certainties. He called all the world's bishops to Rome, for only the second council ever held in the Vatican. Those from the so-called Third World—Africa, Asia, Latin America—stormed the middle class cushioning of the Northern prelates, bringing with them the hunger of their peoples' children, and their cries against the exploitation of their lands.

The monastery began to boil. Suddenly the watchwords were 'Social Action,' 'Reform': above all 'Aggiorniamento,' the bringing of the church into the 20th century.

Suddenly too, faces familiar from daily custom, began to disappear from their places in choir. What were we, vowed to poverty as we were, to make of our huge landholdings?

Our three meals each day? Our certainty of care in old age? What of the new house begun on a scale any rich person might envy?

We who had been so silent were all at once commanded to take all the basics of our life and reevaluate them. Not only in prayer, but also in full community session, during which we were dispensed from our rule of silence. Like sailors stumbling over the unfamiliar stability of dry land, our words spilled clumsily out, eager for excitement, uncertain how to shape it. For many of the older monks it was the first time they had engaged in unrestricted discussion for over 20 years. It brought to the surface doubts and deep criticisms which the silence had bottled up. It revealed how deeply 'functionalism' had bitten into the bone of the contemplative life. Without our shield of obedience, how could we cope with the winds of silence?

We students took to the changing times with all the enthusiasm of our secular counterparts tearing up cobblestones in Paris, or riding the buses in Alabama. Studies were suspended. With so many leaving, we younger monks found ourselves in positions of responsibility which before would have come to us only after years of experience. Mark, a fellow student, and myself became the forestry team. We had our own equipment: we ran our own schedule. Often we would be high in the hills, reworking the outcome of a meeting from the night before as we planted or felled. We became firm friends—a friendship which continues to this day, he still faithfully within the monastery, myself lost to so much that we shared, but still dazed by something of the wonder. I carry him with me in the guitar—we collected the wood for it together.

President Kennedy of the United States was assassinated in 1963. For his funeral we hired a television: the first time ever within the monastery. Once the precedent had been set, the new era saw occasional news items delivered by the reader at our meals; more television (we too were there when the US took its "great step for mankind"). Malcolm Muggeridge—a tame BBC sceptic turning believer—came to use us as a backdrop for his own spiritual quest. He stayed within the community, trying to make sense of our eternal uselessness for TV 'consumers,' locked so tightly into time and things.

Mark and I starred in the end product: a film called "A Hard Bed to Lie on." We personified the monks in revolt, inaccurately presented as hellbent on the destruction of all that our spiritual fathers held dear. Our Warholian 15 minutes came as we were interviewed blithely discussing the sale of the new house for a sanatorium; the need for monks to uproot themselves from their country idyll to take heart back into the modern deserts of the inner cities; and music as perhaps the most appropriate vehicle for contemplation in these changing times. None too subtly we were then captured, as woodsmen, bringing a great tree crashing to the ground.

More enduring were the preoccupations with music and the 'problems' of justice which the Muggeridge programme brought to the fore.

Liberalisation brought a few religious magazines into the library. One carried an article on Joan Baez and Bob Dylan. I got very excited. Trappists sang Gregorian chant. But the choir was awful, sending this subtle music reeling round the church like a punch drunk boxer. It was dispatched at last by the conversion of the whole liturgy into English. The new music was horribly bland: the language soggy. By contrast, the early protest songs stung like salt. They were about real people, real life.

We got a couple of bootleg records, smuggling them away deep within the house. Here we heard "We shall overcome" for the first time; here Bob Dylan's: "Lonesome Death of Hattie Carroll" and "Hollis Brown" and "Medgar Evers."

The times they were a-changin'.

I became consumed with the need for a guitar.

Journal at the Frontline 2

July 28th

Guitar in hand, I've just arrived at this little house, in Highland Park, Los Angeles. One storey, with small yards back and front. A garage which does double duty as storeroom and occasional bedroom. The cars stand in the street. There seem to be about 15 people living here, including half a dozen children. The core of the group is Leticia, mother and grandmother. She has three daughters and two sons living with her. The daughters are married, their husbands are here too, and of course the children.

We're expecting the youngest daughter, Yanira, home today. She's been away 'in the country' for the few long weeks which have passed since she was assaulted by Salvadoran death squads, operating up here in the US with brutal suddenness.

I'm just present as a 'gringo,' to try to provide some sort of protective shield. The various organisations here in Los Angeles concerned with human rights and Central America have banded together to give the squads' chosen targets and other threatened ones some protection. There is a small group of volunteers who come to spend the day and/or night living here. And in other houses marked out for destruction throughout the city. The hope is that, with a white person present, the squads won't attack.

Let's hope that's right.

Who would have dreamed of this? I left Scotland for just three weeks at the back end of April, to come back to

*Washington DC. It was another chance to try to get to
President Reagan with "Blood of the Innocent," the tragic
testimonies of ordinary Nicaraguans living out the
horrible realities of his policy decisions. Last year I carried
this book through all Central America and up to the White
House, only to have the door slammed in my face. (Two of
us from Scotland joined some 300 from all over travelling
from Panama to Mexico on foot and by bus: "La Marcha
por La Paz en Centroamerica: March for Peace in Central
America." It took place through December 1985 and
January 1986.)*

*Astonishingly, April's more than three months ago
already.*

*(Carmen—one of Yanira's sisters—has just brought me
tea. Amid much laughter. My British addiction to
steaming hot tea here in the 100 degree heat is already
quite a joke. And although I speak very little Spanish, and
most of the family little English, food and drink and
laughter reach out, even in such terrible circumstances.)*

*When the paper came round asking for help with this
protective network, I nearly didn't sign it. I was very much
in travelling mode. In Washington DC I met up with a
woman artist, Jane Ford, who had worked in Nicaragua.
She had been living with Brian Willson, of Veterans for
Peace in Central America, when he and some of his
Vietnam friends had started their 'Fast for Life' on the
steps of the Capitol. She complemented their action by
designing and building the 'Peace Hunger Kitchen.' This
was a larger than lifesize interior of a Nicaraguan kitchen.
I'd come back to Washington in 1987 with a delegation
from the many Scottish people who had been in
Nicaragua, to add our challenge to the great
demonstration against the war held on April 25th. Jane*

had set up the Kitchen on the grassy Mall which stretches between Capitol Hill and the Lincoln Memorial. She stayed on there for a week or so, and I wandered in one day on my way back from some abortive foray into the citadel of Democracy. And so I'm here now! What a world!

Jane lives in Vermont, she invited me to come up there to join the Kitchen on tour throughout New England. It was obvious that Washington was closed, so why not?

So: New York, Vermont, New Hampshire.

After a couple of months in the East, over to dip into California, up to Washington State, via Oregon; then back East via Ohio. That was the plan: trying to meet the other side of Reagan's United States: the huge movement of people resisting what their government is doing, of whom we hear hardly anything back home in Britain:

"This song's for you, Uncle Sam—we don't want another Vietnam"

Singing with them, telling them the story of 'La Marcha' and how the democratic White House had refused to listen to the ordinary folk of Nicaragua, by rejecting "Blood of the Innocent" twice over.

I was frightened too.

I only happened to be at the SCITCA meeting at all because of the work I'd done with the churches in Scotland. (SCITCA: Southern California Interfaith Task Force on Central America.) I wanted to connect up with the groups working for the Sanctuary Movement, which gives refuge to Central Americans. Particularly those the state labels 'illegal aliens' (!) who are here as refugees from the repression, and who are now in danger of being sent back by the US immigration authorities.

I watched the list getting nearer, out of the corner of my eye, and with real fear. When we had been in Panama and Costa Rica we were attacked by a death squad style group (Costa Rica Libre), and the thought of deliberately getting back into their path . . .children had been teargassed and one man lost an eye . . . .

But, after all, I was pretty free: just two fixed dates: a concert up in San Francisco at the end of August (Berkeley's famous 'La Pena,' 27th, day after my birthday!); and flying home in October.

Life back home was pretty much messed up. The money to fund my job at SEAD (Scottish Education and Action for Development) ended; and Barbara, my compañera of 7 years, has had to leave.

And anyway what's the good of 'singing of freedom' if you can't respond when the singing has to stop?

Whatever, I signed. And so here I am.

Carmen has reappeared—it's time to eat.

Tortillas, beans and rice: suddenly back in Nicaragua's mountains.

Later

(I've had to be vague with dates, places; some names have to be changed. For security: even 2 years on: here in

the USA. In a way this helps. This journal is a record of actual events, within a particular family and community, and at a particular time. But because stories just like it, and even worse, are the everyday experience of so many people, it happened yesterday, is happening today and will happen again tomorrow.

What makes it special is the crossing of paths between El Salvador and Scotland, here in Los Angeles: the revealing of connections. It is a chance to record one instance of the enduring courage and everlasting hope of many millions of people. And to expose the forces which confront them for daring to challenge those connections. And so to challenge us. Most of their names we will never know, but their great dream—of justice, gentleness and peace—we are all gradually coming to dream: in the slow formation of one people whose allegiance is to our whole exquisite planet and not to the narrow interests of separate nations or classes or the greedy plunder of the transnational companies.)

Yanira has just arrived home, with Carlos her little son. She's young, around 24 I should guess. Very gracious despite all she's been through. She's clearly still in a lot of pain though, and after greeting everyone, has gone through to her room.

Later that same evening

I'm now packed onto a settee in the house of Joanna.

So far she has not been attacked—'only' threatened. And a part of our job is to provide night guard for herself and her teenage children.

Apparently the squads have circulated a whole list of

other people (nearly all women—what courage!) whom they've targeted besides Yanira. Joanna is one of these. It's eery sitting here: someone has wired the television up so that it can be switched to a security camera focussed on the outside of the front door. The picture is not very clear, and its grey emptiness adds to the sense of menace.

Her children are in danger too, although they seem to be almost blasé. They have been brought up here, and so I suppose the horrible facts of life under the death squads in El Salvador are less real to them than to their mother.

Joanna's father was murdered in El Salvador. That's why she got out—to freedom from fear, as she thought. Now this.

Undaunted, she too is carrying on her work, seeking justice for her people.

I must go to sleep. It's after twelve already. What a day. I do hope Yanira and the family are alright.

August 1st

Back in San Fernando with my brother Joe, Paula, his wife, and their two little children. (Joe is actually brother to Barbara with whom I've lived the last years in Edinburgh. She's gone now but Joe remains more than just a friend somehow.)

Amazing how even that little time with the Salvadorans has changed me. Joe and Paula live miles from the city, in a tiny desert oasis hidden away in the hills. Cars hardly ever come by. When they do the road is so rough they have to crawl. The children play all over, inside and out; doors are left open; keys in locks.

Yet the chill of the death squads has made me nervy. I have to lock the door, and check the cars as they grind past. "Children, come in the back please."

Still at San Fernando

Joan called again.

Joan is organising the accompaniment rota. Because I am so free, I left word on her answering machine to say that if it would be helpful I could stay on for a week or so.

She wants me to stay with Yanira and her family— heavens! It seems the rota is made up of many people, from colleges, churches, human rights groups—which is great. But it's exhausting for the family to have a different person to relate to each new day on top of everything else. So Joan feels it would be better to have just one person.

I wish my Spanish was better: and that I was a woman. Apparently Yanira doesn't mind having a man to stay, but . . .

Back in Yanira's house

The guitar is a great hit. Luckily—thanks to Carlos and Sonia and my other Chilean friends, refugees from the bloodbath in 1973, who've taught me so many of the songs of their murdered compañero Victor Jara—I sing Spanish much better than I speak it. So we had a few songs this evening. "Nicaragua, Nicaraguita" is a great favourite, people are very clear how deeply related Nicaragua and

Salvador are. Apparently Sandino and Farabundo Marti worked together back in the twenties, to resist the US dominance of Latin America. Like Sandino, Marti was killed for his resistance. And the Farabundo Marti Front for National Liberation (FMLN) in El Salvador is following in the footsteps of Nicaragua's Sandinista Front (FSLN).

"No Pasarán: They Shall Not Pass"—one of the great anthems of people's resistance. "Por Eso Luchamos: This Is Why We're Fighting" (my only song from Salvador—so far!). The children love it, especially the wee ones: Carlito (little Carlos) and Susanita (3 1/2 and 1 1/2). They twangle away at the strings. Luckily it's only a rough old instrument and not the monastery made one (thinking I'd be here so short a time, I left that at home: I wish I had it now: if ever Soleares made sense, it would be here with this family, with the children).

As on the Central America Peace walk, everyone knows and loves Victor's songs. It's marvellous how music reaches across so many barriers—of language and culture; of creed and age; of politics and fear.

Plus singing with children drives the words home:

*"No olvidamos a los niños que mueren a diario
a lo largo y ancho del todo el país"*

*"How can we forget the children
In every corner of our land—?
They're dying every day."*

(Por Eso Luchamos: Cutumay Camones)

"Si hay niños como Luchin
que comen tierra y gusanos
Abramos todas las jaulas
Pa'que vuelen como pajaros"

"There are so many children just like Luchin
eating earth and worms
Why don't we just open up the cages
So that they can fly free like birds?"

(Luchin: Victor Jara)

2 Echoes of the Weeping Rain

"... and the rain keeps falling like helpless tears"

Just a little rain—falling all around
The grass lifts its head to the gentle sound
Just a little rain
Just a little rain
Oh, what have we done—
to the rain?

Just a little boy, standing in the rain
The gentle rain that falls for years.
and the grass is gone
The boy disappears
And the rain keeps falling like helpless tears
Oh, what have we done—
to the rain?

Just a little breeze—out of the sky
The trees nod their heads as the breeze blows by
Just a little breeze
With some smoke in its eye

Oh, what have we done...?

**(What Have They Done To The Rain?
(adapted): Malvinia Reynolds)**

News came through of Birmingham, in Alabama. Of
Addie May Collins, Denise McNair, Cynthia Wellsley and
Carole Robertson. And the bomb which blew them to bits
at their church on "Birmingham Sunday." This was one of
the first songs we learned. The bomb had been placed
because the congregation was black. Because Rosa Parks
and Martin Luther King, Jr. were claiming back their
people's pride, Jim Crow was going beserk.

"...and the choir kept singing of freedom." How that
refrain haunted us:

"In the old Baptist church there was no place to run:
and the choir kept singing of freedom.

"The preacher who spoke was a man they all knew:
and the choir kept singing of freedom.

"Her thoughts and her prayers would have shamed
   you or me:
and the choir...

"Young Carole Robertson entered the door
And the number her killers had written was four
She asked for a blessing—she asked for no more:
and the choir kept singing of freedom."

It's good to sing, especially of freedom.
But what happens next? How *could* we stay hidden
away? What were we doing living in such splendid
isolation, when the world was catching fire? And why were
the Parkses and Kings the exceptions? Where were all the
other church people? Where had we been while the fire was
building? Where had we been while the slaves were being
offloaded in Carolina and Maryland, and the gold in
Liverpool and Bristol and Glasgow? Where were we now,
when it was becoming clear that that appalling gold had

helped buy us world dominance? And, with that dominance, the land and labour and lives of so many of our
'brothers and sisters in God'?

It was a period of enforced inactivity which brought these
questions home to me.

The enforcement came in the shape of a large tractor. I
was driving but told myself that Brother Fillan needed help.
He was throwing swedes off the trailer behind; we were
feeding cattle. I got off to lend him a hand. Really Fillan and
I were rivals: he was better at philosophy, I could drive
tractors. To show how good I was, I could control the
monster even from the ground. Yes sir!

In getting back on it's probably better *not* to get your foot
caught under the wheel. Everything happened as though to
someone else. The great wheel lumbering on, pulling me
down and under; the strangely elongated groan as the
breath was squeezed out by the remorselessly advancing
weight; the quiet, calm knowledge that I was going to die.

And then, unbelievably, the lifting of the pressure.

It turned out that Fillan could drive tractors as well as
out-think Aristotle. Just as well: he took me to the hospital.
All I suffered was a massive ankle strain and a wrist which
still creaks under pressure. Plus bruised pride and weeks of
rest.

"...And the choir kept singing....". What else were
we doing? What was the good of all the songs, all the
preaching about 'love' and 'justice'? If it was by our fruits we
were to be known, then what...?

As farmers we were increasingly tied into the greedy,
anti-contemplative world of agribusiness. Besides trying to
squash us, the tractors' noise, fumes and dominance of the
land cut us off from much that had shaped the early monks.
They had worked as peasants: with simple tools in their
hands, the perfumes of the land in their nostrils. Our

machines, wonderfully though they could alleviate drudgery, battered and pulverised the land into submission. So the natural rhythms and times were distorted.

As Christians we stood accused by history.

We had murdered and pillaged, enslaved and raped. In the name of Christendom we had outsavaged those 'savages' we came to 'civilise.' We had trampled down the cultures of so many peoples: seizing their food land for our drugs: tobacco and coffee and cocaine; destroying their families and communities for our slaves and servants; replacing their gods—sensitive to the delicate local environment—with our single god, who dealt in universals and cared little for their bodies as long as their 'souls were saved.' *We* were the four horsemen of the apocalypse, enseeding plague and war into the land.

Nor were the plagues over. Our modern society simply could not function without that dependency on cheap raw materials from the land we had stolen. Land where families used to grow their children's food. Parasitic advertisers taught us to get fat on expense accounts and chocolate (and thin again on foodless foods and trim gyms), while the people who slaved over the coca (or tea, or tobacco) struggled for 15 hours a day just to stay alive—on what had been their own land. We made up about 20% of the world's people; yet we were sucking in 80% of the world's resources. While our pets and our children went on diets to combat the junk food and the cola, their children bloated out, dying with pellagra, and the dogs scavenged the remains.

California

It's early morning, and little Susanita, clutching her blanket, has settled sleepily on my lap. She often does this: Carmen and Antonio, her parents, left for work long since.

They have to work all the hours there are to make ends meet, and they can be 'terminated' at a moment's notice. All around here other little children are being left. It makes me angry to go over to Hollywood or Beverly Hills, where the fat white children loll, and the Cadillacs stretch like cats in the sun—the toys of the greedy grown-ups.

And there are so many churches: "...the choir is still singing of freedom."

Three things happened. I renewed my temporary vows; made a guitar; and fell in love with Catherine.

Normally the choice had to be made: stay forever in final, ineradicable vows, or leave. However the storm of renewal was so intense that the juniors of our changing times were offered further temporary vows. Not everyone accepted this extension—Mark for one. He went on serenely, taking his final vows like a gull, lifting in the wind.

He's the novice master himself now.

For me, however, there was no other possibility. And once again I knelt before the solemn conclave of monks, my hands joined between those of the abbot, and asked for his blessing for 3 more years.

The questions did not stop. The need for a guitar grew.

Even if such a 'modern' instrument were to be admitted, no individual monk had money, and no matter that I might think the monastery rich, it had no money for such dubious investment.

My parents probably had. But how could I ask for anything? One hundred dollars would have bought a good guitar then. But $100 would have kept most families in the world fed for months. And the guitar was to sing their song.

That anguishing over money gave me the most creative

act of my life. I *had* to have a guitar. I could not buy one. I made one. That simple act taught me so much about myself, about the false 'expertisation' of our society, about the beauty of wood and tools and creativity, that I only wish we were challenged to the inventions of necessity more often. For that creativity lies in us all. Only it's largely distorted, used by the tyranny of consumerism to keep us passive to forcefeed us at will.

I found a broken drawer on the rubbish tip. Using this as the body and a chunk of window framing for the neck, I cobbled away until a crude guitar was fashioned. The family *was* pressed into service for the strings (either this compromise or gutted cats!).

The end result? Not elegant—but it worked: enough to start learning to play. It made me determined to make a proper instrument. Back to the rubbish tip for more treasure: a broken table leg became a beautiful mahogany neck; the face was the bottom of another old drawer; the sides were scraps of flooring from the new chapel. The 'capo'—to raise the pitch—started out as a toilet seat. Mark and I cut down a tree of Spanish chestnut, and a slice just covered the back.

This went on, surreptitiously, over months, while everyone else prayed.

The times were now running complete riot. Monk after monk left. The other 3 novices, the students. Senior monks were going too. People who'd been in the monastery for years. By the late 60s, hardly a month went by without yet one more gone.

Most left in anguish, certainties, home and friends gone all in the one. Some left the priesthood altogether, others tried to settle into parish life as curates. One or two left in association with women.

I was one of these.

The new house was being built with the help of many craftsmen, during their holidays. They lived in a former prisoner-of-war camp in Garvald, the village below our land. Any women who wanted to help worked as cooks (they weren't allowed alongside the monks on the house). Catherine was one. I was given the job of driving the builders up to the site, and one day she just climbed into the van. I was delighted. I'd seen her several times before, and there was a shimmering whenever our eyes met.

We went to where I was clearing trees. We sat quietly on the hillside, listening to the gentle wind, talking about the life; SHELTER, the organisation for the homeless, with which Catherine worked; about her atheism. This was hardly wisdom at work, but things were so confused, and I was already so changed that there was little chance of my staying.

On the way back, she straddled a barbed wire fence. Compromising situations no. 1! It was a measure of our attraction that the careful operation I had to perform to free her caused so little embarrassment.

Catherine returned to her life in Edinburgh, and I was left with lovely memories, a couple of letters, and even more unanswered questions. The monks were marvellously tolerant of my goings on (especially given the turmoil of their own lives). And Mark was constantly at hand to discuss, challenge, question, support. Together with Francis, another young monk also tormented, we made a natural threesome, each helping the others to face reality, to take care for the baby as well as dispose of the bathwater. Francis is a teacher now in England; I'm on the way to El Salvador; Mark remains. However far apart we've moved our friendship remains, and we still turn up on Mark's doorstep every year.

The music was too strong.

The day before I left the monastery for good, the new guitar sang its first note. It was sweet and true. Twenty years later we're both still singing.

I went to Catherine. It had been more than 12 months since we had last seen one another. We had written sparingly, to allow space to find the true path. But when the choice lay made, there was only one person to go to, one question ready answered: "Do you love me?"

We went to live in London, sharing the tiny flat she and Pat, her sister, used in Pimlico. By wonderful chance, the SE London Oxfam office had a vacancy: Bromley, Kent. Within weeks I was working there as assistant regional organiser, driving Pat's little bullnose Morris up and down.

There could have been no greater contrast: from the gently paced life among the rolling quiet of the empty hills to the chaos of Oxfam, the cut and thrust of the fume-choked streets of London. To say nothing of the ménage-a-trois after ten years' celibacy in an all-male company. But there was no strain: only excitement and expectancy and coming home.

Oxfam was *the* Third World Charity. It shared the ideology of the time, when the immense scale of world hunger was just beginning to hit home, for *us* at any rate. The 'problem' was people over there without food, the 'solution' was people over here giving something of our surpluses, of money and of food. The naive expectation was that, with enough donations, the world would be transformed and all the starving children fed.

Daphne, the organiser proper, worked all hours. She led from the front. These were the early days of the OXFAM shop. Many of ours were just jumble sales, glorified. That involved persuading chain stores to let us use an empty shop, filling it, finding volunteers to staff it, and rolling in as many people as possible before closure caught up with us. On the road from morning to night, we had to fix shelves and cart rags, present slide shows, sooth ruffled helpers, write letters to the press, speak on radio. Chaotic, but hardly dull.

Always I was trying to work with the music. To begin, simply to gain sufficient skill and self-confidence to sing in public at all. I was *not* a natural. When my brother, Joe, had married, back before the mountaintop, I had been so terrified as best man that *he* had had to help *me* climb into my top hat and tails! And someone else had to be pressed into giving the speech at the reception.

It was the monastery of 'silent' monks which had cured this oversensitivity. Passions had run so high during 'the revolution,' that public speech forced itself out of me despite my terrified self. A more forbidding context for maiden speeches could hardly be imagined. The monks' chapter, or meeting, was always conducted with such set seriousness. And the Abbot was quite deaf when the debates began, so *any* question, however mild, sounded hostile because we had to shout. My knees used to knock, literally. But the matters being discussed were so vital, somehow embarrassment was self-indulgent.

This was still more so when people's lives were at stake. So, soon I was performing regularly, using the homemade guitar as a conversation piece to engage people, and zapping them, once hooked, with the most miserable protest songs I knew. I had a lot to learn. I remember a 'young mother' coming to me after I'd given it to her group with both barrels. "That was wonderful, Paul," she said, "your voice was so gentle all the babies fell asleep." *Not* an indignity to which Master Dylan was ever subjected, I'll bet!

Just as monastic life had taken a battering during that last 10 years, so now challenges were being thrown down to many other organisations. People began to ask the harder questions. Was the spasmodic application of band-aids really what this Third World needed? Presenting people with surplus food might keep them alive for today, but what did that sudden influx mean for the small farmers trying to produce food for tomorrow? The typical OXFAM supporter would have "nothing to do with politics," so could we engage in a critical analysis of British government policy without losing them?

We needed to be challenged: 'No politics' was too facile. Daphne was clear:—to be serious, OXFAM and the other agencies *had* to grasp the nettle: most of the 'poor' people for whom our liberal hearts bled weren't poor just by chance. There were deadly political games going on. In many countries, especially those only recently freed from overt colonialism, there were elites, usually educated in the North, who had moved in to take the colonists' place. They were vital links in the chains of colonialism—arms-length, controlling the people through the police and the armed forces, to make sure that foreign capital would see their countries as good risks (and that they would make their fortunes). The Shah in Iran. Somoza in Nicaragua. Duvalier in Haiti. Smith in Rhodesia. Franco in Spain. And we were all implicated: our grandfathers had taken the peoples' lands and tried to blot out their cultures; our fathers had trained the *monigotes* — the puppets of pseudo-independence; we were living on the fat they had stored up for us, and, claiming it as our right, defending ourselves to death against change, against justice.

The people were not just 'the poor,' they were 'the disinherited.' And we, for all our supposed good works, were with the disinheritors.

This was news that we did not want to hear. It called into question Oxfam's whole being. We went begging to the descendants of the very people who had stolen land, labour and life itself from the families of the starving children weeping on our posters. We worked very hard, but were we any different from the missionaries we criticised, who had done appalling things, in the name of their God of all love? We lived as northerners within the North. While most of the world's people lived in hovels and walked—or crawled—we, obedient consumers all, bought our houses, our cars, our insurance—just like the Joneses. We filled our refrigerators with the fruits and meats and drinks of slavery, and our children's stockings with Christmas junk produced in the sweatshops of poverty. We were not different. The secular choir sang just as offkey as the ecclesiastical when the chips were down and real freedom, justice, was on the table.

Again for me this was driven home through music and poetry. I joined the pilgrimage to the writings of the indigenous people of North America: the so-called Indians:

"When I was a child I knew how to give—
I have forgotten this grace since I became 'civilised.'

Every pretty pebble was valuable to me then—
Every growing tree an object of reverence.
Now I worship with the white man before a painted
    landscape
whose value is estimated in dollars:
just as the natural rock is ground into powder
and built into the walls of modern society.

The First American believes profoundly in silence
The absolute poise of body, mind and spirit.
To him, the unlettered sage,
silence is the ideal attitude and conduct of life:
Not a leaf, as it were, astir on the tree
Not a ripple on the surface of the shining pool.

If you ask him: 'What are the fruits of silence?'
He will say: 'They are patience, dignity,
true courage and endurance—
For silence is the cornerstone of character.'

If you ask him: 'What *is* silence?'
He will answer: 'It is the Great Mystery—
The holy silence is his voice.'

(Oksaya: Oglala Sioux: from "Touch of the Earth")

Then the guitar—above everything the flamenco.
Shortly after finishing it I developed a sore throat.
Unable to sing, I found the guitar was singing to itself: a
mysterious, marvellous smouldering of sound which
somehow sang all the centuries of silence and love. Lorca
comes closest:

"Empieza el llanto de la guitarra—the cry of the
guitar begins:

It is useless to hush it: it is impossible to hush it.
Unending as the water weeps...it weeps for things
  far away
Sand of the warm South...asking for white camellias
It weeps: arrow without target, evening without morning
wind over the snowfall
And the first dead bird upon the branch...

Es inutil callarla, es imposible callarla..."

Crude echo though it was in my untutored hands, this
song of the still silence captivated me. Only afterwards did I
learn that what had searched me out was the root of all
Cante Hondo—the 'deep song' of the flamenco: 'Soleares'—
'the songs of solitude.'
    The echoes of this eternally weeping beauty sang in my
deepest self, wherever I was, whatever was happening. It
was not morbid, it bore its own healing within the weeping.
Again who can speak these silences? Again it was the great

silence of love, the point where life and death become one
mystery, where sorrow and joy make lasting sense only in
one another's arms.

Living with Yanira and the family I have seen that
mystery, because they have looked death directly in the face.

Our civilisation (was it Gandhi who said: "Yes, it's a good
idea; what a pity it's not been tried yet?"), with its
idolisation of painless consumerism, can't cope with pain
and fear and old age and death. It has pills for its pain, and
locks for its fear; 'homes' for its aged and blindness for its
death. And so there is little real joy, real laughter, real
loveliness.

"But if in your fear you would seek only love's peace and
love's pleasure
Then it is better for you that you cover your nakedness
and pass out of love's threshing-floor
Into the seasonless world where you shall laugh,
yes,
But not all of your laughter
And you shall weep,
yes,
but not all of your tears."

(The Prophet: Kahlil Gibran)

Ultimately, in disinheriting the earth and the peoples of
the earth, we are dispossessing *ourselves*. We can no longer
bear the silence, we resist any reality that hasn't been cut
down to magazine style and weight and sacrificed to the
flickering god, gibbering in the corner of every living room.
All our lives shrunk to this little measure. We immunise
ourselves against the demands of reality: real pain and real
joy and the involvement they call for. We trivialise
ourselves to death.

The rain weeps for us.

Journal at the Frontline 3

My job seems to be to be as visible as possible.
Apparently the squads frequently come and just sit in their
cars across from the house, watching. They followed
Yanira from here when they attacked her the first time (a
month before the rape they ran her off the road and tried
to drag her into another car. She was beaten up pretty
badly. And wee Carlos was with her in the car, watching it
all. They stole her purse. A few days later a photo of
Carlito, which had been in the purse, arrived through the
post, with the threat to kill him.)

So I'm writing this sitting against the garden fence,
hoping they don't come by with a machine gun. The other
children, who thankfully don't seem too affected by all
this, are rampaging about on the lawn. The street is quiet,
just the occasional car, and one or two persons on foot.

The weather is so hot! Eighties, 90s, even 100 now! If
we get one week back in Britain with the occasional 80
we've got a good summer. Fortunately there's a tree which
shades almost the whole of the front. It's not very big but,
as the sun goes round, I can follow the shade across the
grass until, at the end, I'm leaning comfortably against this
chainlink fence.

I feel very bad that my Spanish is still so poor, but
everyone is being very kind to me, and at least Yanira and
a couple of the others speak OK English. We don't see
much of her though. She's clearly been very badly hurt,
and has to keep to her room most of the time. (Apart from
the fact that they raped her with a stick, they kicked and
beat her, and cut her hands and tongue.) Luckily I brought

"Spanish in Three Months" with me from home—on the spur of the last moment—so now I can have no excuse for not getting down to it in earnest.

Talking of home, I have to start another "Letter from the Frontline"—I'm trying to write an extensive letter home every month to keep the people in the networks in touch. We'd no idea that this sort of thing was happening. I wonder how long it'll be possible to keep it up from here on in.

Plus I have the concert to prepare up in San Francisco. It's at the famous 'Peña,' in Berkeley. At the end of the month. I can't really believe it even yet. Within revolutionary song circles 'La Peña' is quite a mecca. Ever since Victor and his friends set up their peñas in Chile, before they were slaughtered in Pinochet's CIA-supported coup. ("Peña" means something like "ceilidh," that's Gallic, helpful hey?!: "gathering": "sing-in": "shared concert.")

Spoke to Joe on the phone last night. Great, a bunch of letters at San Fernando for me to collect. People are writing constantly, being very supportive. I hope there's some more money, I'm beginning to run low.

So, back onto the so-called 'Freeways' (they seem everlastingly clogged with traffic), in this great boat of a car. Joe and Paula are being wonderful: lending me their second car. The laws seem very complicated here—I'm not even certain that my British licence allows me to drive. But, what the hell; without a car you're finished. Los Angeles is just so sprawled out and the public transport so poor.

I can't get over the volume of traffic. No wonder this

place is buried in smog so much of the time.

"What have *we done to the rain? What* are we doing . . . ?"*

August 3rd

The phone rings constantly: often there's no one on the other end. I'm supposed to intercept all calls, but whenever she's up Yanira herself picks them up. Sometimes they're silent with her, sometimes there's dreadful laughter, sometimes they repeat their threats: to get her again, to kill Carlito. Yanira refuses to let them prevent her from answering her own phone, either through injury or through continued threats. The family seems more concerned to protect her than she does herself. She exudes amazing spirit, winking at me as she whisks the receiver up from under my nose.

On top of everything else, the entire family has to move. Ever since the attacks happened, it's been obvious that they can't stay here, especially with the threats to the children. Everywhere there are boxes standing: years of their lives spent together here in this little house, packaged away to go who knows where? Or even when?

Joan has been trying to get hold of another house. But it's hard: how to find somewhere big enough for so many, with a rent which can be managed—(There's a group of students at one of the local colleges (Pomona) who have pledged themselves to find funds for paying that, for three months. That's great, but even so.)

I do hope she can come up with somewhere soon: the phone threats, the people sitting outside like vultures, the possibility of attack: all these are bad enough. On top, *having to leave, and yet in limbo, with nowhere to go.*

Two days on

Joan has just phoned. We have a house!

*So now, the exodus. Antonio, Carmen's husband,
brought a huge truck by, the drive-it-yourself kind. And
with determined haste we filled it within a couple of
hours. No sign of panic: just relief that at last everyone
can get away from the brooding menace. Luckily the new
house isn't too far away, so we could make several trips,
both in the big van and in several smaller pickups. In this
way the whole moving operation didn't take more than an
evening. And Juan, one of the sons, is staying on in the old
house (with the family's big, fierce dog!) to keep the lights
going and to make the place look inhabited still.*

    *We kept a good look out of course, but with that huge
truck standing in the driveway, the whole neighbourhood
must have known we were moving. As far as we could tell
none of the death squad cars came by, and we weren't
followed. But how can we be sure?*

In the new house

*So this is our 'safe' house. ¡Ojala! (Oh let it be!) We
came in the darkness. It's only now, the following
morning, that we can see what an extraordinary place it is.
It's huge: gigantic rooms, high ceilings, 3 bathrooms, big
garden and garage. Obviously I can't write down where it
is, in case I lose this, or it gets stolen somehow. But,
whereas before we were in a real 'población,' 'people's
quarter,' this is the land of the 'ricos muertos': people
seemingly entombed in their wealth.*

Next to Joan it's the students at Pomona that we have to thank for the house. Not only are they paying the first three months' rent, but John Cooper, who has been co-ordinating their work, apparently asked his parents could we use it. They bought it to fix up, to sell again. While that's happening, we can stay. ¡Que bueno! John's parents are Frank and Elizabeth, they run a law practice from their home. Apparently Frank will be calling by a little later today. They must be good people. It's a big risk to take: the house is their investment after all, and it's not inconceivable that the squads will burn it down.

August 8th

We've quickly settled down. As befits our new neighborhood, the house is quiet compared with the constant coming and going at the old one. The address and phone number are being kept secret so, for all that the family still has to live out of boxes and they don't know where they'll be in a few months' time, they should be able to begin a little peace.

My time here is supposed to end tomorrow, but there's no way I'm going: it might be different if I had a schedule to keep, specific people to meet. How can I leave Carlito and Susanna just to go travelling on?

I must phone Joan to let her know.

3 For Those Who Died Screaming

"Levantate, y mira la montana . . . hoy es el tiempo
que puede ser manana!"

"Stand up and see: the wonder of the mountain
Source of the sun, the water and the wild wind. . .
You who can harness the rush of mighty waters
You who, with the seed, sow the longing of your soul

Stand up and see: the hands with which you labour
Stretch up, grow tall, hands joined with these your brothers
Working together, by deepest blood united
Knowing together: the future can be now!

Free us from those who weigh us down with misery
Bring us your kingdom of justice and equality
Blow like the wild wind through the flowers of the mountain
Cleansing like fire the barrel of my gun!

Give us this day a world where no man is master
Fire us with your strength and honour in the fight
Blow like the wild wind through the flowers of the mountain
Cleansing like fire the barrel of my gun!

Stand up and see: the hands with which you labour
Stretch up, grow tall, hands joined with these your sisters

Working together, by deepest blood united
Now
and in the hour of all our deaths
Amen.

(Plegaria a un Labrador: Victor Jara)

Astonishingly, for Scotland, the sun was blazing down.
The crowd, gathering since morning, stood at 300,000,
the largest ever in Scotland's history.

Bellahouston Park, Glasgow, June 2nd 1982: Pope John
Paul II was concluding his first ever visit to Britain with an
open air mass.

From the stage the scarves and banners and faces
stretched away for ever, swaying slowly to the massed
singing of "We Shall Overcome." Onstage we were as
motley a collection of nominal Catholics as he would ever
meet. Sheila was a 'Traveller,' a singer from the wandering
people of Scotland; Frank, unemployed, had just outwalked
us all as we carried three huge crosses the 40 miles through
from Edinburgh, his feet toughened from pounding the
pavements in search of work; Giovanna and Carlos were on
the run from Pinochet's torturers in Chile. Each was to sing,
and speak, of their own experience of injustice. I was to link
the presentation together, to lead the singing.

All of us stood aloof from the traditional church: long on
words, short on action.

Our allegiance was to the growing movement for peace
through justice, church-based or not. We were 'seizing the
time,' in Bobby Seale's phrase. Asked to address this
enormous congregation, who needed theological debate
when there was homelessness and unemployment and
repression to fight? We had one brief half hour before the
Pope himself came on. We had to make the most of it.

Our crosses, with their stark messages, carried our faith: "People need food, not more weapons: Homes, not more weapons: Work, not more weapons."

It was an exhilarating day, a landmark in the long struggle to bring poverty and war into confrontation with our Christianity of comfort, defended to death by the weapons of mass destruction. To catch a glimpse of the faces buried in the statistics of disaster. To grasp how we were all—at home too—being sucked into a world system which spat used people out like gobs of chewed over gum. Not only were we killing the natural world, we were using up its people. The culture of consumerism had rendered people down to disposable things.

The music of Carlos and Giovanna especially set us on fire.

Thousands of miles from their homeland, separated from their families, in flight from the torturers, they sang not only of their sadness but also of their hope—their determination to go home one day, when their country would be free. The gigantic crowd was captivated: somehow, from their dreadful experiences—far worse than anything we were ever likely to have to endure—these lone Chileans brought *us* comfort, laughter and life.

Afterwards they were in great demand. We did several concerts together. And from them I began, above all, to learn Victor's music, he of the gentle hands and lovely songs:

Victor Jara of Chile
Lived like a shooting star
He fought for the people of Chile
With his songs and his guitar

His hands were gentle, his hands were strong

Victor was a peasant

He worked from a few years old
He sat upon his father's plough
And he watched the earth unfold.

His hands were gentle, his hands were strong

When the neighbours had a wedding
Or one of the children died
His mother sang all night for them
With Victor by her side

His hands were gentle, his hands were strong

He sang for the copper miners
And those who worked the land
He sang for the factory workers
And they knew he was their man

His hands were gentle, his hands were strong

He grew to be a fighter
Against his people's wrongs
He took their joys and sorrows
And turned them into songs

His hands were gentle, his hands were strong

He campaigned for Allende
Working night and day
He sang: "Take hold of your neighbour's hand:
The future begins today!"

His hands were gentle, his hands were strong

When the generals they seized Chile
They arrested Victor then

They caged him in the stadium
With five thousand frightened men

His hands were gentle, his hands were strong

Victor sang in the stadium
His voice was clear and strong
He sang for his fellow prisoners
Till the guards cut short his song

His hands were gentle, his hands were strong

They tortured him for two long days
They beat him on the head
They broke the bones of both his hands
And then they shot him dead

His hands were gentle, his hands were strong

The generals still rule in Chile
We British have our thanks
For they rule with Hawker Hunter jets
They rule with Chieftain tanks

His hands were gentle, his hands were strong

Victor Jara of Chile
Lived like a shooting star
He fought for his people of Chile
With his songs and his guitar

His hands . . .

(Victor Jara of Chile: Adrian Mitchell/Arlo Guthrie)

I've sung that song a hundred times: it still brings me to the edge of tears. Victor has become a hero throughout the world; his songs and his story are heard wherever there is a gathering of people working for change. We sing them in Scotland, and we sang them in Panama, in Nicaragua and in Mexico; 'internacionalistas' we met there knew them from Australia and New Zealand, India and Japan.

His story is so moving not only for the beauty of his music or the appalling waste of his destruction, but also because his life and death write large the story of so many thousands of unknown people, everywhere, struggling to bring justice and to make peace against the gigantic odds. And because what he left us is not sadness, but strength and inspiration and courage for the gentle fight.

He was a remarkable person. Born into a poor peasant family, he wrote of his drunkard father: "I remember my father as a hole in the wall" ("**La Luna siempre es muy linda: The moon is always very lovely**"). His mother, Amanda, was left to find most of the family's living, working so hard that she died of a heart attack at 50. For her he wrote one of his tenderest songs: "**Te recuerdo, Amanda: Amanda, I remember you.**"

Amanda, I remember you
Running through the soaking streets
Running to the factory
Where Manuel worked.

Your smile radiant
The rain in your hair
Nothing mattered
You were going to meet him
To meet your Manuel

Just five minutes with him
Life was eternal just for five minutes

The siren sounding calling back to work
And you walking
Bringing light to everything
Those five minutes
Had made you flower.

Amanda, I remember you
Running through the rain soaked streets
Running to the factory
Where Manuel worked

Your smile radiant
Rain in your hair
Nothing mattered
You were going to meet him
To meet your Manuel

And he had gone to the mountains
He who had never hurt
Had gone to the mountains
And,
In just five minutes,
He was destroyed
The siren sounds still, calling back to work
Many have not come back
Among them Manuel

Like many of his songs, this was born within his own
family (one of his daughters was also called Amanda), but
it's also inseparably about his poor Chile, her beauty broken
by the dominance of the foreign companies, and the desperate fight forced on those who try to break that
dominance.

Victor put himself through university. He worked in
theatre and dance, and quickly became one of the leading
lights as a director. His graduating play, *Animas de Día*

Claro (Spirits of Bright Day), won an award, and brought him fame in the wider community. His work's exploration of the struggle for social justice, and especially his directing of Brecht's *The Caucasian Chalk Circle,* brought him the unwelcome attentions of the reactionary forces, both those governing the university and those in power in the land. While studying, he met his English wife, Joan, who was teaching dance and movement. She had come to Chile some years earlier, having married a Chilean dancer in Britain. He left her just after the birth of her first child, Manuela. Desperately depressed, the teacher was reluctant to accept the advances of one of her students. But his gentle concern, for herself and for Manuela, gave her back her courage, and, in due time, they married.

With Joan, and other friends, he broke out of the academic world. They began to write community drama, using dance, speech and music, and toured throughout Chile, performing in little halls, in the open air, in cafes: wherever people were. It was the experience of these journeys, through some of the poorest parts of Chile, which brought their anger to white heat, and their little company put itself at the service of the Movimiento de la Unidad Popular (Movement for Popular Unity), a political movement, trying to bring in a people's government under the leadership of Dr. Salvador Allende.

One of the revelations of working with the Chileans was to find how important poetry and music and dance are within their culture. This has been repeated time and again in Central America, and here with the Salvadorans. Carlos Mejia Godoy, Nicaragua's Victor Jara, remarked, famously: "The contras will never win, because they have no good songs!" He's not just speaking of the death of the creative spirit among mercenaries. He's also invoking the deep humaneness of a culture where people still have time to stop and *listen.* Where the standard harangues of political gatherings are interwoven with the more demanding subtleties of poetry and music.

Drama had always been Victor's first love. At first he only sang as a pastime. But the music began to take him over, and song after song flowed with him, the lives and deaths of the poor people he was meeting again mirroring his own experiences as a little boy.

"I am moved more and more by what I see around me . . . the poverty of my own country, of Latin America and other countries of the world; I have seen with my own eyes memorials to the Jews in Warsaw, the panic caused by the Bomb, the disintegration that war causes to human beings and all that is born of them . . . But I have also seen what love can do, what real liberty can do, what the strength of someone who is happy can achieve. Because of all this, and because above all I desire peace, I need the wood and strings of my guitar: to give vent to sadness or happiness, some verse which opens up the heart like a wound, some line which helps us all to turn from inside ourselves to look out and see the world with new eyes."

(Victor: An Unfinished Song: Joan Jara)

A cultural cafe, (a peña), was started in Santiago, and there Victor would sing, joining others of the growing New Song movement: Quilapayun, Angel and Isabel Parra, their famous mother, Violeta, Patricio Mans. It must have been a wonderful time, filled with ferment and challenge and the slow growth of astonished conviction that Allende's party might one day make it to office (His Government of Popular Unity was elected in 1970). They worked to resist the insidious imperialism of moron musack and gibbering disk jockeys beamed down by the North—the racket of emptiness indeed. They took their Chilean culture and built on it their New Song. Their music challenged the 'protest movement,' as we "kept singing of freedom." Victor said:

"You sing songs of protest: great, keep singing. We have to *live* songs of revolution: join us." For him there had to be complete integrity between the music and life, both political and personal.

One of the most endearing things was that he refused to be taken in by the infantile 'Superstar' bandwagon: he had no fancy car, he didn't sing: "imagining no possessions," from the comfort of his private mansion, sitting at his grand piano, kept from his people by high walls and gangs of guards. He had no need to imagine: his stomach remembered the gnawing hunger, his ears ticked with his mother's exhausted footfalls dragging into the dawn. He could see the children scrabbling for food, picking over the garbage. Far from hiding from people, he took his songs directly to them: to those who would join him. And to those who would kill him:

Stand up and see: the wonder of the mountain
Source of the sun, the water and the wild wind
You who can harness the rush of mighty waters
You who, with the seed, sow the longing of your soul

Stand up and see: the hands with which you labour
Stretch up, grow tall, hands joined with these your sisters
Working together, by deepest blood united
Knowing together, the future can be now!

So he sang with his fellow campesinos.

For the others, he had questions: **"Preguntas: por Puerto Montt: Questions for Puerto Montt"**

Very well then, I will ask:
For you and for you and for him
For you who are left alone
And for him who died without knowing

He died without knowing
Why the bullets smashed into his breast
While he was struggling for his right
To a patch of ground to live on

How unhappy that man
He who ordered the shooting
Knowing very well how to prevent
Such a foul massacre

You must answer, señor Perez Zujovic
Why they came against an unarmed people
with guns
Señor Perez, your conscience is buried in a coffin
All the rains of the south
Will never wash your hands clean

He died without knowing
Why the bullets smashed into his breast
When all he was struggling for
Was his right to a piece of land
To live on.

He sang this to 100,000 people in Santiago, after government troops fired on families taking over unused land near the little town of Puerto Montt.

"Why must we beg for charity, our children go hungry, on this land—*our* land before it was stolen?" And, doggedly, a few here, a family there, they had repopulated that desolation beyond all others: land left to lie idle because the landowners do not find it profitable to use.

They planted their scrappy crops, waiting on the time.

In the morning, very early, the soldiers came and the "población"— the people's settlement—rang with fire.

The song became a scream:

Puerto Montt! oh Puerto Montt!
Puerto Montt! oh Puerto Montt!
Puerto Montt! oh Puerto Montt!
Puerto Montt! oh Puerto Montt...!!
Where are you—
my poor people...?
my poor ones
my Puerto Montt...?

He didn't stop there. He went with a poet friend to sing
and read at a public school. He usually allowed the event
itself to suggest the songs. But, knowing the school, open
only to the rich, they chose material to challenge the
students to look over the walls of their privilege. A group
was waiting: among them the son of Perez Zujovic himself,
the Minister named in **Preguntas por Puerto Montt** as
responsible for ordering the killing. They shouted insults.
Victor went straight into **Preguntas**. Stones crashed onto
the stage, hitting both men and nearly breaking Victor's
guitar...They had to be smuggled out....
   It was probably this song, with its fearless naming
names, which marked Victor down, for which, when the
time came, they killed him so brutally.

After his death, Joan, back in England, received a video-
tape, apparently made clandestinely when Victor was in
Peru, a few months before the coup. Jan, an Edinburgh
friend, who lived in Santiago and knew Joan and Victor
well, has a copy. We watched it together. There was a
marvellous sense of stillness about him, sitting calm on a
high stool in the studio, wearing his poncho, cradling his
guitar. He spoke simply, quietly, humorously, answering
questions. And his songs made his answers fragrant.
   He could read the times as well as any. Jan says he
probably knew what lay ahead, what his likely fate would be.
   Faithfully he went back. And on September 11th 1973,

when the North's 'democratisation' process entered its final phase, unleashing the brutal war against the elected government and unarmed civilians, he was trapped in the inevitable fascist sweep through the centres of creativity and thought. They found him at the university. Joan's beautiful book tells, with heartbreaking simplicity, of coming to the campus days afterwards, to find their little Renault standing forlornly, alone in the car park, as Victor had left it.

They took him to the stadium where he had sung so often. Now, with Allende destroyed in the ruins of the presidential palace, the triumph of 'Democracy' over 'Communism' blotted out the songs with screams as the torturers restored their law and order to those who had dared to vote for another way.

When they discovered who they'd caught, they set "that fucking singer" aside for special treatment. They broke his hands, piece by piece, bone by bone, inch by inch. "And then they shot him, dead."

There are five thousand of us here
In this little part of the city
I wonder how many we are in all
In the cities and in the whole country?

Here alone are ten thousand hands which plant seeds
And make the factories run
How much humanity exposed to hunger, cold,
Panic, pain,
Moral pressure
And insanity.

Six of us were lost
As if into starry space:
One dead
Another beaten

As I could never have believed a human being could
    be beaten
The other four wanted to end their terror
One jumping into nothingness
Another beating his head against a wall
But all with the fixed stare of death.

What horror the face of fascism creates
They carry out their plans with knifelike precision
Nothing matters to them
Blood equals medals
And slaughter is an act of heroism
Oh God
Is this the world you created?
For this
Your seven days of wonder
And of work?

Within these walls only a number exists
Which does not progress
Which will slowly wish
More and more for death.

But suddenly
My conscience awakes—
I see this tide has no heartbeat
Only the pulse of machines
And the military showing their midwives' faces
full of sweetness

Let Mexico, Cuba and the world cry out against this
    atrocity
We are ten thousand hands
Which can produce nothing
How many of us in the whole country?
The blood of our President will strike

With more strength than bombs and machine guns
So will our fist strike again!

How hard it is to sing
When I must sing of horror

Horror
which I am living

Horror
which I am dying

To see myself
Among so much
And so many moments of infinity
In which silence and screams
Are the end
Of my song.

What I see
I have never seen

What I have felt
And what I feel
Will give birth
to the moment...

This is Victor's last poem, unfinished. He scrawled it in the stadium. Friends smuggled it out after the guards came for him the last time.

Journal at the Frontline 4

August 12th

I'm trying not to ask too many questions, but am beginning to piece together what they did to Yanira. First, about
two months ago now, she and Carlito were going to Los
Angeles airport—a long drive, mostly on freeways.
Towards the end she began to be aware that a car behind
had been changing lanes consistently as she did. As she
went down the off ramp it swerved up beside her car and
crowded it into the side. Two men jumped out, wrenched
her door open and began dragging her out. Although she
was beaten badly she managed to hang on until they were
frightened away by someone stopping to help. Carlito was
in the back all the time, screaming. They were North
Americans apparently.

They took her purse, and, to begin with, she thought it
must be a robbery. But a few days afterwards—wait!
Ranger, the dog, is barking, I must go and see . . .

Nothing, it's OK.

A few days later she got the letter with Carlito's picture
which had been in the purse, threatening to kill him
unless she stopped her work.

Then, July 7th, just as Joe and Paula were driving me to
San Fernando from the airport (how weird that is, how
could we not have known? How could people have been
driving within feet of the van, and not have felt something
awful was happening inside it?), she was kidnapped from
outside the CISPES office (Committee in Solidarity with
the People of El Salvador) in downtown Los Angeles.

*Three men this time: all Latinos. They forced her into a
van, and, as they drove around the city, they tortured and
raped her (with a stick!—I just can't get over that:
castrating men is standard death squad practice in El
Salvador. It's that same ghastly attempt to destroy all new
life. Yanira's certainly so badly wounded inside that it's
not likely that she'll be able to have more children).*

*They even argued back and forth over her battered
body, whether to kill her outright. In the end, said they'd
let her live to serve as a warning to everyone else—but if
she didn't stop . . . Then they threw her out.*

It makes me ashamed to be a man.

*The policeman who found her harrassed her, and we've
just seen in today's papers that the Chief of Immigration
in this part of California: another man: Harold Ezell, has
gone on record claiming that the whole kidnap/rape was a
put up job to get publicity and sympathy for the FMLN
cause in El Salvador. Can you believe it? How distant do
these people have to be from the reality to be able even to
think such things? (This 'Leftists carry out atrocity to
frame government forces' story is being used increasingly
as a tool of disinformation: no wonder people are
confused.)*

*The FBI, on the other hand, which has had to be
pressured even to investigate the crime, has been taking
the line that rape is an everyday occurrence in big cities,
and that Yanira has to show them the assault was
politically motivated before they'll get involved.*

*Even walking upright is still a terrible struggle for her,
she certainly can't drive. How they expect her to get out
and find the sort of proof they want, they haven't
explained. Nor how they propose to warm the trail up*

again, growing colder by the minute, in the unlikely event that she does eventually succeed in convincing them.

August 14th

This evening we were all sitting around, singing. Yanira joined us halfway through, sitting quietly on the end of a sofa. She didn't smile, although her lips were moving on one or two of the songs. At the end she asked simply: "Please, will you sing 'Mi Venganza Personal'"?

"Oh I will be revenged upon your children,
When they've the right to schooling and to flowers
My vengeance will be sweet when I can sing you
This song born in the freedom and the quiet hours
My revenge will be to show you all the goodness
I see shining in the eyes of this my people
Courageous and unyielding in the battle
But still more constant and more generous in the victory

When that day comes I'll greet you with 'Good Morning'
And there will be no beggars left to haunt us
For you, my brother, I can demand no prison
But call on you to clear your eyes of sadness
For when you the one who tortured me stand forward
Your eyes downcast and all your strength forgotten
My revenge will be to reach to you, my brother
With these the very hands which once you tore and tortured
Without the power or strength to
rob them of their tenderness."

She was really smiling when I finished, really smiling.

Who needs commentary? "Mi Venganza Personal—My

Own Revenge" was written by Tomas Borgé. One of the original Sandinistas, he was tortured, and his wife was killed, by the dictator's National Guard. He wrote the poem for his torturers. I learned it in Washington DC, after hearing it sung at a memorial service for Ben Linder, the US engineer killed in El Cua, Nicaragua, by the contras. He was the first US civilian to be killed. He dared to be bringing water and electricity to remote villages. Because he was in a war zone, and may have had a rifle at his side, US Secretary of State for Inter-American Affairs, Elliott Abrams has called him a legitimate target. Sure, set up a mercenary army to destabilise a government, seen as genuinely elected by all independent observers (including those of your own allies!); let it loose in remote regions of a peaceful country to terrorise civilians; when the people, for safety, take up arms to defend themselves, designate those areas 'war zones'; kill anything that moves.

And of course the hands reaching out always bring Victor's ruined hands back to life: at once 'so gentle and so strong':

> *"Even in a state of shock, my body continues to function. From outside I look very normal and controlled . . . my eyes continue to see, my nose to smell, my legs to walk . . .*
>
> *We go down a dark passageway and emerge into a large hall. My new friend puts his hand on my elbow to steady me as I look at rows and rows of naked bodies covering the floor, stacked up into heaps in the corners, most with gaping wounds, some with their hands still tied behind their backs . . . there are young and old . . . there are hundreds of bodies . . . most of them look like working people . . . hundreds of bodies being sorted out, being dragged by the feet and put into one pile or another, by the people who work in the morgue, strange, silent figures with masks across their faces to*

protect them from the smell of decay.

I stand in the centre of the room, looking and not wanting to look for Victor, and a great wave of rage assaults me. I know that incoherent noises of protest come from my mouth, but immediately Hector reacts. "Ssh! You mustn't make any sign . . . otherwise we shall get into trouble . . . just stay quiet a moment. I'll go and ask where we should go. I don't think this is the right place."

We are directed upstairs. The morgue is so full that the bodies overflow to every part of the building, including the administrative offices. A long passage, rows of doors, and on the floor a long line of bodies, these with clothes, some of them look more like students, ten, twenty, thirty, forty, fifty . . .

. . . and there in the middle of the line I find Victor.

It was Victor, although he looked thin and gaunt . . . What have they done to you to make you waste away like that in one week? His eyes were open and they seemed still to look ahead with intensity and defiance, in spite of a wound on his head and terrible bruises on his cheek. His clothes were torn, trousers round his ankles, sweater rucked up under his armpits, his blue underpants hanging in tatters round his hips as though cut by a knife or a bayonet . . . his chest riddled with holes and a gaping wound in his abdomen. His hands seemed to be hanging from his arms at a strange angle as though his wrists were broken . . . but it was Victor, my husband, my lover."

(Victor: An Unfinished Song: by Joan Jara)

Victor, Tomas, Ben, Yani: all these wonderful people bonded together in the one song, dreaming the one dream.

It makes me so angry when people say: "Yes, but aren't they 'political'?"

Even if they were, does that somehow make murder, rape, mutilation permissible? What do we mean? "Yes but ....?"
'Political'. How that word used to frighten me too. It has been tainted—hijacked by the disinformers.

Of course *they're political: they have to be: children without food are political: schools shut down for lack of funds are political: US mines in Nicaraguan waters are political: the death squads finishing the work begun by the military are political. There is a world order which supports political systems which are responsible for these outrages against fundamental human values and life. So people like Yanira are forced to be political. The threat they pose is that they want to redeem politics from the politicians and the forces which control them—the dreamers of little dreams—and return them to "us, the people" (Not Marx: The US Constitution). For real politics are our lives: the art of people living together in all our diversity. And dreaming together.*

While I was in DC Martin Luther King's birthday was finally declared a national holiday.

"I have a dream today!"

I often take the little guys—Hector and Juan—to school: a school which has Chinese, Salvadoran, Vietnamese, Korean, Black, White children. The dream is (very) partly here.

Yanira doesn't want to be President. All her 'politics'
are built into that one great dream: that everyone *should*
be able to live at a decent level, and everyone be free to
dream.

I wrote this poem:

Just one more day: breakfast and then school
One more checking out the children's lunchbox.

Just one more day to dream
to work
to hope—
willing on and on
the one great dream.

Great dream? Yet not so much:
That every child may one day have a lunchbox?
With food to put inside it, day on day?
That every child indeed may have a school
to bring that lunchbox to?

A simple dream, no more

My sister is a simple woman,
walking, dreaming,

simply.

Behind her the darkened van draws close:
Unmarked
—and unremarked.

4 For Those Who Laugh in the Darkness

" . . . and we are dreaming, dreaming for our lives"

We are a gentle, angry people
and we are singing, singing for our lives
We are a gentle, angry people
and we are singing, singing for our lives

We are the builders of new visions
and we are dreaming, dreaming for our lives
We are the builders of new visions
and we are dreaming, dreaming for our lives

We are young and old together
and we are working, working for our lives
We are young and old together
and we are working, working for our lives

We are the weavers of new patterns
and we are weaving, weaving for our lives
We are the weavers of new patterns
and we are weaving, weaving for our lives

We are a gentle, angry people
and we are singing, singing for our lives
We are a gentle, angry people
and we are singing, singing for our lives

(Gentle, angry people: Holly Near)

The presentation at Bellahouston was a highpoint in all the years struggling and singing for justice, since Nunraw. OXFAM also gave way to the music in the end. I needed more space than the endless demands of Daphne's shops could allow. The choice was clear, stay on and forget the music, or follow it one more time...

We came to Edinburgh. Catherine went to work with the British Volunteer Programme, which sent unpaid workers to Africa and Asia. I ended up as a milkman.

'Confessions'? Forget it. There was no time for dalliance. We started at 4:30 and grudged every second. The milk put up the money for my share of the household and, provided my wretched customers didn't catch me hurtling past, time. For the guitar; for working with the anti-poverty agencies, as a volunteer; and to begin a first book: *Of Minstrels, Monks and Milkmen.*

Burning to change the world overnight, I forgot the needs of my partner. Soon Catherine and I were grabbing for a few comatose minutes before I collapsed into bed, to make ready for the sprint start. (How to learn that caring for those who're close—and for ourselves—is also part of the revolution?)

After three years I could bear it no longer and took to subsisting on welfare to try to make my way as a musician and writer. I was hopelessly unprepared, understanding nothing of the simple endurance which they both demand from all but the immensely talented or exceptionally lucky. Nor the erosion of dignity which welfare spreads like a contagion. My courage and my clothes soon wore thin. Catherine's patience with me ran out. We split up. Guitar in hand I was back on the road.

Ironically, my next home was an abandoned convent, in a desperate housing estate. Just what I'd been proposing as a monastic gadfly. The nuns, rehearsing our own arguments of monastic revolution, had become uncomfortable in their comfort, set down in the midst of such need. They had taken local council flats to be more genuinely among their people. I'd joined Edinburgh's Young Oxfam group and, while doing the usual things to raise money for projects, we had concluded that, to be serious about making justice happen, we also had to change our day-to-day lives. They were deeply meshed into the lunacies of consumerism. We helped perpetuate injustice with every cup of tea we drank. So were looking for a flat together, to begin to practise a little of what we preached. The YWCA (Young Women's Christian Association) invited us to live in the convent, which they were converting into a hostel. We would caretake while the work was done, they would not charge rent.

Fine. The snag was that everyone else had a place to stay already. I ended up alone, incarcerated in the echoing shell (built for 16), with the local children running riot round and around, smashing the windows and tweaking the doorbells with relentless randomness.

Naively I imagined that the solitude would help me complete *Of Minstrels, Monks and Milkmen.*

Instead it brought on a relapse into despair. And this time there was my abandonment of Nunraw and Catherine to add to the fire.

After a horribly lonely 9 months—without a note sung or a word written—we found a flat: the young Christian women moved into the hostel. I was moved out.

Once again the new place reeked of dead clerics. Forlorn and empty in a dirty dead-end street it had once been a church school. The pipes had been stolen, the windows shattered, but we moved in anyway, fixing as we went. To sum up our philosophy (such as it was) we called ourselves 'Sharing in Development Group' to stress the need to receive as well as to give, and 'Shindig!' for short and for the parties born of friendship.

We weaned ourselves off meat because of the callous fattening of the calves of consumerism on poor peoples' grain. We rode bikes, helped set up a co-operative to import Nicaraguan coffee, used our rents (Shindig owned the house) to fund projects. It was the guitar over again, worked into the fabric of daily life: food, work, home ownership, money.

Another temporary job appeared, with Scottish Education and Action for Development (SEAD).

SEAD set out to do the political education and campaigning work that OXFAM was forbidden. Scotland had clawed its way into the finals of the World Soccer Cup, in Argentina. Under the slogan "Football: Yes! Torture: No!", we mounted a campaign to use the sudden hype to focus on the disappearances and murders carried out by Argentina's military government. I was to help with routine office work, for the duration of the finals, freeing the permanent workers to concentrate on the campaign.

It was of limited success, the spotlight chopping off after Scotland's abrupt collapse at the first hurdle (one newspaper ran the headline: "Football: No! Torture: Yes!"). Jackie, whose place I'd taken, decided to stay with the Latin American movement, and resigned from SEAD. I became Community Groups' Organiser.

I worked part-time. As ever this was to try to keep space for the guitar, which had weathered all the storms, though only just. Many times I almost abandoned playing, especially after Catherine. But the music clung on to me, somehow, especially the Cante Hondo, pulsing in very blood.

I was still leftover from the 60s. "Where Have All The Flowers Gone?," "Blowing in the Wind," "We Shall Overcome"—were my stock in trade. The spirit had gone out of music in the 70s. The anger had been tamed, sucked into the commercial music business, or discarded as no longer relevant. We'd carried guitars before, to share the music, now people were autistic, wired into the 'personal stereo,' drilled into electronic uniformity.

Flamenco aside, it was the music of Victor and the rest which broke me out of my timetrap, and made me, irrevocably, a musician.

Chile and Nicaragua and El Salvador still lay in the future. SEAD mined the idea that Scotland too was in some ways a Third World country. International companies, having used its people to get started, were pulling out, to use the cheaper labour of India or Taiwan. The shipbuilding had collapsed, the iron and steel factories were shutting down, the cars were rolling away. Huge tracts of Dundee, Paisley, Glasgow were left to rot as the gates clanged shut. More and more coal mines were declared uneconomic. Even fishing and farming, the immemorial occupations, were shutting out the small people, as the tentacles of 'agri-business' clutched the land and swallowed up the seas. We ran campaigns on tea and cotton, against Finlay's and Coates Paton. And to resist the looming Trident nuclear submarines, bringing world destruction to brood among the beautiful Scottish islands. Our supposed defence was other people's real disaster: the world simply hadn't the resources for both the weapons and the children.

Because of my past and remaining tentative affiliation, much of my work was with the churches. The great vision of a world freed from the stranglehold of weapons and hunger should fit naturally into the religious frame. Wasn't our first concern with those for whom in President (General) Eisenhower's words: "Every gun that is fired, every tank that is built represents the theft of food"? ("Lord, when did we see you hungry, or thirsty, or homeless, or naked?") And weren't we supposed to have a faith which "cast out all fear," and so couldn't religious people dare to take the long view, whatever the risks?

Sadly those questions still hang over the churches.

A year after Bellahouston the lightning struck again. On September 23rd, 1983, a delegation gathered in Crathie church, across from Balmoral Castle. 10:30 am, a beautiful morning. We had come to lay an 'open letter' before Queen Elizabeth II, in Scotland, at her holiday home. Nobody had ever done this before.

The focus of our anger was the imminent deployment of Cruise, in Britain and Western Europe. The British government was arguing that 'our' weapons' systems needed to be modernised to counter 'the Russians'' build up in Eastern Europe. The peace movement said Cruise, with its first strike capability (by stealth), undermined the deadlock (by threat) of "Mutually Assured Destruction" (MAD!), on which peace and security were supposed to rest. And it was the first of a new generation of weapons which, including the monstrously accurate and powerful Trident, would escalate Britain's nuclear power 1000-fold.

The storming of Balmoral was a marvellous combining of the pressure of the times—and luck.

We began the journey to the gates of one castle camping out under the walls of another. Princes Street, Edinburgh's main thoroughfare, lies directly below the huge castle rock, rearing up in the centre of the city. To the west stands a tall, dark church: St. John's. In the early 80s it became a centre of peace action, under a new Rector: Canon Neville Chamberlain. (He and the British Prime Minister's famous "peace in our time" remark arrived simultaneously. Unhappily, by the time Hitler was smashing into Poland, Neville was irrevocably christened.)

We heard of an international group who were fasting openendedly to challenge our governments' priorities in upgrading their nuclear weapons while reducing their assistance for those without proper food. We set up a support fast each Saturday. Neville and his church gave us our base; we coaxed passersby to stop and write messages of encouragement to the fasters, and "We don't want Cruise or

Trident" cards to the government.

The real fasters drew close to 60 days without solid food, and still we hadn't even made the local papers. I was given the job of drawing up an open letter to the government, which we would invite leading clergy to sign and the press to publish. It was to be signed right there on Princes Street.

Our best hope was that a few leftwing folk would respond, and that, at last, we might crack our hometown daily.

Just before the signing, I picked up a surprise call. Michael Hare Duke, one of the Episcopal church's most forthright bishops on making peace. "We like the statement, Paul," he said. "With a bit of amendment, I think we could get our bishops' conference to back it. We're meeting tomorrow; would you mind if I changed it here and there, and took it to the other bishops?"

Would I mind?!!

The following evening he was back. "We did it, Paul. The whole conference signed the Letter. Also, again I hope you don't mind, but we sent a signed copy on to the Roman Catholic bishops—they'll be having their conference next week."

Mind!!?

Suddenly the phone was redhot. Before we knew it, leaders of all the main denominations had called in their support, many of them pledging to take part in the public signing.

So far, so suddenly good.

We realised we could go for broke. Wasn't this especially the *Scottish* church community in anger? Didn't the Queen make much of her Scottish connections? Hey!—Wasn't she in fact up in Scotland already, for the traditional family holiday together at Balmoral? So she was not supposed to be approached on political matters, but we'd gone to the government, repeatedly, with scant success. Why shouldn't the Scottish churches go to her, as Head of State, to tell her just how impossible real dialogue with 'Her Majesty's Government' was under Mrs. Thatcher? The Iron Lady had her 'defence of liberty' bit well and truly between her teeth in the wake of her jingoistic bullying of Argentina (Las Malvinas). Her gunboats had probably saved her from political extinction, and she was seizing *her* time to railroad the missiles in.

Such a venture would also give the churches, increasingly loud in their condemnation of continued reliance on ever more powerful and/or more accurate weapons, a chance to act together.

Let's try it!

We had a line of senior bishops, Moderators of whole churches, and General Secretaries of councils of churches. The spark had fallen just when the brush of so many withered hopes had reached explosion point, and the winds of all our anger were reaching storm strength.

Getting to Balmoral was tricky. Here were church leaders whose programmes were filled months in advance, expecting me, a renegade monk with no official church standing and a highly dubious faith, to pull a top level delegation together in less than a week. It had to be top level, from all the main Christian denominations. *And* the taboos around Balmoral had to be broken plus the Queen persuaded that the iron rule preventing the interruption of the monarch's holiday had to be set aside.

It says a great deal about our anger at the northern governments' betrayal of the world's peoples, that crossing two such minefields should even have been attempted. And that such people, bound in by the subtle chains of rank and position, should have come so emphatically off the fence.

Since leaving Nunraw I'd been out of the official church. This may have been a good thing, since, all unaware of crosscurrents and protocols, I banged on cardinals' doors and rang moderators up, ignoring the jungle of ecclesiastical divisions and committees. Almost at once a couple of leaders said they'd drop everything else for Balmoral, and we were on our way.

Balmoral itself was much tougher.

Getting the telephone number of the castle was surprisingly easy: it took one phone call to Buckingham Palace, the Queen's official residence in London. There a secretary calmly recited the number for me, without question or comment. She also gave me a name: Robert Fellowes, one of the Queen's secretaries: Democracy reigns! Democracy perished, or very nearly, in the miasms of suavely deployed avoidance tactics which followed! It was one thing to phone Mr. Fellowes at Balmoral, quite another to get him to answer, or to ring back. For someone on holiday he proved to be everlastingly busy, and call early, call late, he was ever engaged, or out, or...

I might have given up. But for a slip one of his own secretaries made. "Mr. Fellowes is still out on the grouse m...: er, he's still out, busy; I'm sorry." The thought of this man swanning about the Highlands blasting away at little birds, while our part of 'mankind' was taking another giant step towards blowing the whole beautiful world to bits; and of the millions of families for whom such supposed sport would be an obscene waste of infinitely precious food, set my blood on fire.

It came down to the day before. The signing ceremony had been no problem, even the pouring rain, which had been falling for a week, switching itself off for just that one day. We'd made the Edinburgh "Evening News," and radio and television besides: the plan to storm the castle at Balmoral, with such unexpected troops, had broken the block and the newshounds were packing on the scent.

Now we had to deliver.

It was only on that last day that the final delegate came into line.

And at last I spoke directly to the sporting Fellowes. Bad news: "Mr. Baker, I have to say to you that you are wasting all these important people's valuable time. There is absolutely no question of any delegation being received at Balmoral. Her Majesty is here on holiday. The proper place to approach her with such matters is London, at the Palace."

There could be no turning back now. We yelled at one another: "We're coming anyway!"/"I warn you, you will not be allowed in!"

Thank you and Goodnight!

It takes three hours to drive to Balmoral from Edinburgh, and we all had plenty of work to do without wasting a whole day visiting locked castles. So before leaving I repeated an (expletives deleted!) version of my discussion with Mr. Fellowes. Bishop Haggart, who as Primus ('first among equals') had led his church up out of the dreary flatlands of compromise, over peace and justice, snorted, and loaded us into his car. The consensus was: "If they won't let us in, we'll just stand outside until they do!"

So there we were, that beautiful morning: two bishops, a former Moderator, a President, a General Secretary, a Chairperson or two—and a folksinger. They embodied the conferences and assemblies of all the principal Christian churches in the land. Accustomed to high level life, they were in top persons' attire, ranging from the pinstripes and topcoat of formal ministerial costume to the sporran and kilt of fulldress Highland wear. I had to borrow shoes, pants, a shirt. I was impressed by everyone's tolerance: it was nervewracking enough to be committed to visit reluctant monarchs by maverick former monks, without having them come along as walking ragbags.

The television cameras were already there, and rolling, and the quarter of mile's walk between church and castle entrance was gratifyingly strewn with 'media' people, jockeying for the best angle.

The gates stood open, but they were cordoned across by police. We were ready to stand in vigil for the rest of the day. However, two men in plain clothes came cautiously out from behind the cordon, and approached us.

Within seconds Dr. Reid and myself were in a sleek police car, whispering up the long drive to the castle.

We'd done it! It was actually happening: we had breached the walls, the years of tradition, the intransigence. Apparently the Queen herself had cut across the resistance of her staff: Mr. Fellowes informed us, via the two at the gate, that "Her Majesty commanded him to say that she had agreed to accept the Letter. *And* that the leader of the delegation, plus the organiser, were to be granted access to the castle."

We hadn't actually organised a "leader": the enterprise was remarkable enough for its bringing together of churches which a few years earlier had been at one another's throats. This organiser wasn't about to get into the minefield of which dignitary should be designated leader. I turned it over to the others. Dr. Reid got the overwhelming vote: as representative of the national church, as Queen's Chaplain, and as holder of the Military Cross. It was probably the addition of his name at the last moment (he had been yesterday's final delegate) which broke the impasse.

It was hard to concentrate on the surroundings, beautiful though they were. The drive cut through a forest of tall, gracious trees, that I do remember. As we passed, police persons kept popping out from behind the trunks. It was quite comical: these were London 'bobbies' wearing their traditional tall helmets—a forestgarden peopled with truncheon wielding gnomes. As we swept smoothly by each helmeted head would ping up, withdrawing quickly at a wave from one of our companions.

The car rolled into the sunlight, luminous on the

cultivated lawns, and there was the castle.

Balmoral is quite discreet, especially by contrast with our home castle, grimly dominating the city. It's a very large country house, with a minimum of castellation and a maximum of windows. We drew smoothly in at the foot of a flight of stone steps. At the top stood two footmen (police officers?) dressed in traditional livery, holding the doors open. We were ushered through the vestibule, across a wide corridor, and into the lion's very den: Mr. Fellowes' own office.

He was more mildmannered than the phone had led me to expect. Smiling cautiously, he came forward: I stumbled introductions. Dr. Reid, veteran of a thousand ceremonies, made a delicately timed speech, short and sweetly rehearsing the body of the Letter: how the churches were united in opposition to the new generation of nuclear weapons: not only did they escalate the chances of a first strike, but they distorted the future with fear and suspicion, and diverted human intelligence and material resources away from humanity's great needs; how they were urging the government to build for the future instead by helping to feed, house and educate the people of the world; and how that government was simply refusing to listen to any dissenting voices, for all that they were so many, and from so many sectors of the community. He brought the churches' greetings to the Queen, and their regrets that the refusal of the government to behave democratically had made it necessary for them to come to her, even in her holiday home. These matters were so deeply of life and death that they simply could not be held back until she returned to London. He knew she would understand. And with a courtly bow, he handed over the Letter, with all its illustrious signatures appended.

Mr. Fellowes, in his turn, made a few polished remarks of acceptance, how Her Majesty had commanded him to accept the Letter on her behalf; and to lay it before her immediately; how much she appreciated the deep concern shown by the churches; and how she would respond appropriately in the near future.

All this over, everyone relaxed. Together with the London bobbies, the court had packed its English tea, and, with a wave of the Fellowes' hand, more footmen appeared carrying silver trays, teapots, cups and all the rest of the paraphernalia of Empire. Even biscuits.

Next minute, he and Dr. Reid were deep in reminiscences of army life! It turned out that they had both served in the Scots Guards, the one as junior officer, the other as colonel, before taking to their respective highroads. The whole thing became almost surreal: here we were on the churches' most impassioned foray ever into peace, and it was turning into an old soldiers' reunion!

At last I managed to remind them of the bishops and general secretaries cooling their heels outside, and we were conducted back to the stone staircase, where, footmen standing rigidly to attention as before, we reloaded into the police car. Mr. Fellowes shook our hands, handed us in, and waved prettily as the car drew away.

The others had not been left idle—the television and other news media crews had descended on them in swarms, and while we had been drinking tea and discussing old comrades at arms inside, they had been recording interviews.

This unprecedented incursion into the Queen's privacy made national headlines, and the interviews were broadcast throughout Europe. The BBC world service carried the 'Balmoral Letter' story, and friends from as far afield as New Zealand wrote in support.

Next day three of us went to take a copy of the Letter to Mrs. Thatcher, at 10, Downing Street; and to the Houses of Parliament, at Westminster, with copies for every Member of Parliament.

In time the Queen replied, thanking the churches again

for coming to lay their concern before her, and, as expected, saying that the nature of the issues raised meant that she had to pass the Letter on to the Government. However her Christmas message that year brought an angry outcry from that same government because she laced her usually careful remarks with allusions to the underlying problems of world injustice, calling on all nations to band together in eradicating poverty and reducing arms' buildups. Many people felt that the departure was so startling, and the themes so akin to those expressed in the Balmoral Letter, that there had to be a connection; and that it showed how moved the Queen had been. Let's hope so.

We didn't turn Cruise back, not then at any rate—it was way too late for that. But the Letter was one more step in the buildup of resistance to those values which put the defence of sanitised greed before people's lives. Thousands of people wrote in to SEAD to associate themselves with it, and it gave a tremendous boost to my work over the next years, which included similar delegations even into the hallowed headquarters of NATO and SHAPE in Brussels to argue the arms versus human resources case (and to sing anti-war songs in the officer's Mess). (NATO: North Atlantic Treaty Organisation; SHAPE: Supreme Headquarters Allied Personnel Europe.)

Thankfully, this, together with the many other events they had inspired around the world, convinced the original fasters that their action had been effective. They started eating again. Most of the 12 had fasted more than 60 days, just taking water and some fruit juice. Their health was badly affected. They all recovered in the end, some more, some less.

The political effectiveness of the Letter was shown by SEAD being called to account by the Thatcher government. Her administration reluctantly provided us with a token grant—an anomaly bequeathed them by the previous socialist administration. They threatened to cut it off. But in the end it proved too difficult for them to withdraw: we had the backing of too many people and the story had become too big.

We survived, just. The 'gentle, angry people,' from Greenham to Balmoral, was on the move with all the beginnings of irresistibility.

OPEN LETTER
from the Churches of Scotland regarding H.M. Government's attitude towards the Arms Race and World Hunger (1983)

All major churches in Scotland have spoken out against the escalation of nuclear weapons.

The British people now face a situation in which, with the concurrence of their government, Cruise missiles are about to be deployed on British soil.

The government is pursuing this course in the face of serious and informed opposition from people in all sections of society.

Apart from the churches' statements, there have been repeated demonstrations of a size never experienced before in Britain (some in excess of 500,000 people); millions of people have put their names to petitions to halt deployment; canvassing and letter writing have been undertaken by peace groups which have mushroomed up and down the land. Opinion polls have shown that probably half of Britain's population is against the deployment of Cruise. (One poll, MORI 22/1/83, puts the percentage as high as 61%).

The government does not appear to have taken seriously the widespread concern that efforts should be directed towards reducing the level of armaments rather than increasing new weapon systems. There has been no significant response to the arguments put forward, not only by peace campaigners, but by many military experts that the increasing weight and sophistication of weapons heightens insecurity rather than produces stability.

Although the proposed deployment of Cruise missiles has caused a sharpened perception of our dangerous situation, the forward planning for a whole new generation of nuclear arms needs to be called into question. We appear to be locked into an unalterable assumption that the hostility between the super powers will continue indefinitely. We are planning for a 21st. century which will be characterised by the same unresolved, aggressive confrontations.

Because of our commitment to Christ and our faith in the purpose of God for His world that He has created, we are compelled to place all our actions within the context of His intention that we should live as one family, able to find forgiveness and reconciliation between each other in the world.

We therefore urge that a positive policy of international aid and development should replace the attempt to achieve security by an escalating arms race. At present we commit enormous sums of money, vast quantities of material resources and, most vitally, the creative lives of many of our front rank scientists and engineers to this spiral of destruction. Yet, Britain has not yet honoured its promise to provide 0.7% of gross national product to aid for countries in need.

For many people in the world there is not a future threat of destruction. It is happening now. Hunger kills as surely as any weapon. Because of the waste of world resources many are denied their rightful share of food, clean water, good health, shelter and education.

We are further aware of an increasing tendency for those in government to avoid serious public debate and instead to attempt to denigrate or marginalise those who oppose them. In this we discern part of the danger which arises from a reliance upon deterrence through a threat of destruction. Decisions of life and death become concentrated in the hands of fewer and fewer to whom any questioning of authority is unacceptable.

We, leaders of the churches in Scotland, therefore request our government:

1. To engage in serious debate about defence issues, including the deployment of Cruise missiles, with those who seek alternative ways of security.

2. To give priority to opening the channels of communication and understanding between East and West so that tensions arising from false perceptions may be reduced.

3. To honour at once this country's promise to contribute 0.7% of GNP to proper and genuine Aid and Development for the poorest countries, ensuring that such assistance be not tied to trade, except where trade is clearly to the advantage of the truly poor.

SIGNATORIES TO THE OPEN LETTER
(in order of signing)

Bishop James Monaghan, *President, Justice & Peace Commission, Roman Catholic Church in Scotland (and entire Episcopate, including Cardinal Gray)*

Very Reverend Malcolm Clark, *Dean of Edinburgh (on behalf of the Primus and all the Bishops of the Episcopal Church, whose names appear later)*

Ellen Moxley, *Religious Society of Friends*

Reverend Ronald Ferguson, *Leader, Iona Community (and on behalf of Lord George MacLeod)*

Reverend Gerard Hand, *Professor of Moral Theology, Roman Catholic College of Drygrange*

Duncan MacLaren, *General Secretary, Scottish Catholic International Aid Fund*

Canon Neville Chamberlain, *Rector, St. John's Episcopal Church, Edinburgh*

Reverend Duncan Forrester, *Professor of Christian Ethics, New College, Edinburgh*

Margery Turnbull, *representing Anne Hepburn, President of Women's Guilds, Church of Scotland*

Helen Steven, *Society of Friends*

Reverend Andrew Morton, *Church of Scotland Overseas Council*

Edwin Lucas, *Fellowship of Reconciliation*

Very Reverend George Reid, MC, *Former Moderator of the Church of Scotland*

Paul Baker, *Organiser with Scottish Education for Action and Development and representing Reverend Ernest Cairnduff, Director of Christian Aid in Scotland and Dr. William McGuire, Director of Oxfam in Scotland*

Reverend David Humphries, *Episcopal Theological College, Edinburgh*

Reverend John Dalrymple, *leading writer and broadcaster on Catholic spirituality*

Canon Kenyon Wright, *General Secretary, Scottish Churches' Council*

Reverend Alan Horner, *Chairman of the Methodist Synod in Scotland*

Joyce Gray, *President of the Congregational Union in Scotland*

Bishop Mario Conti, *President of Scottish Catholic International Aid Fund*

Bishop Derek Rawcliffe, *Episcopal Bishop of Glasgow*

Bishop Edward Luscombe, *Episcopal Bishop of Brechin*

Bishop George Sessford, *Episcopal Bishop of Moray*

Bishop Frederick Derwent, *Episcopal Bishop of Aberdeen*

Bishop Michael Hare Duke, *Episcopal Bishop of St. Andrews*

Bishop Alistair Haggart, *Primus and Episcopal Bishop of Edinburgh*

Reverend Columba Ryan, OP, *Leading Moral Theologian, Roman Catholic Church*

Reverend Donald MacDonald, *Principal Clerk to the General Assembly, Church of Scotland*

Reverend David Lyon, *General Secretary, Overseas Council, Church of Scotland*

Reverend Andrew Morton, *Secretary for Churches and Ecumenical Relations, Church of Scotland*

Christine Davis, *Clerk, General Meeting for Scotland of the Society of Friends*

Cardinal Gordon Gray, *Archbishop of St. Andrews and Edinburgh*

Bishop Morris Taylor, *Roman Catholic Bishop of Dumfries & Galloway*

Bishop Charles Renfrew, *Roman Catholic Bishop of Glasgow*

Archbishop Thomas Winning, *Roman Catholic Archbishop of Glasgow*

Bishop Vincent Logan, *Roman Catholic Bishop of Dunkeld*

Bishop Steven McGill, *Roman Catholic Bishop of Paisley*

Bishop Joseph Devine, *Roman Catholic Bishop of Motherwell*

Bishop Francis Thomson, *Roman Catholic Bishop of Motherwell (retired)*

Journal at the Frontline 5

August 15th

I've just finished a letter to Scotland, asking for money. I hope people will understand. Money is another taboo, like politics: Ask me for my life—just leave me my money. And people in the justice and peace movement don't often have a lot of cash. But we must get another car for Yanira. She's clearly determined to go on working (cf: article from LA Weekly below). She's been doing lots of interviews and speaking engagements. When she can't borrow a car, she still uses the old Ford Capri the squads caught her in. They almost wrecked it: it's got a whole wing missing, and sounds awful. So, maybe we can get a little, nondescript kind of car, which will be reliable and cheap to run. Here's hoping . . .

August 26

My Birthday. 48. Ouch!

Much to my delight the family bought me a cake! And we had an interesting version of "Happy Birthday To You." The tradition here (I suppose because it's so warm) is to go for a light sponge mix, rather than the good old British heavy fruit job. It was very nice, and, with so many of us, soon wolfed away. Mother and Father and everyone in Britain were right on time too: got about ten cards all today! Pretty good, hey?!

Wonder where I'll be next birthday? I'm already beginning to think about trying to extend my visitor's permit for a further 6 months from October. Somehow being here makes so much sense of everything that's

*happened up to this; and of all the songs. So many people
my age have to start thinking: retirement. Here I am, just
beginning.*

*It's frightening, a bit: I wonder about Shindig. The
others in the community back in Edinburgh are worried:
Am I ever coming back? They're holding my room for me,
but that can't go on for ever. It's a large, light room, the
best in the house really. Plus, including me, half the
members have moved on since I left Edinburgh, and the
new group needs time together to find its own coherence.
It does* not *need a spare part 6,000 miles away!*

*But it's scary to think of giving Shindig up. It's been my
home for 10 years now . . .*

*I got a letter: "Can I tell them what I'm going to do?"
It's only fair, I suppose, although it seems a bit hard: so
much going on here at this frontline. I feel angry
sometimes: can't they see what a fight we have on our
hands?*

*But I know that's not fair. It's not a different war—just
a different front. They're struggling with unemployment;
the new discrimination of the taxes against the poorer
folk; to come closer to a balance between women and men;
trying to develop a creative and non-exploitative way of
life over against consumerism and the bomb. I miss my
friends; the whole food; the intelligent balance; the
growing garden.*

*I'm still scared, but I think I will give up 'my' room.
Living here, within this extended family, is* community:
the Salvadorans haven't lost the art.

August 28th

This is a bit wobbly—I'm writing on a Greyhound bus,

roaring its way back down from San Francisco.

La Peña was a flop! Oh no! Hardly anyone came, and the PA system was ghastly—it kept fading in and out. What a shame! I hadn't realised it had such a fantastic regular programme—something on nearly every night. And, of course, who the heck is Paul Baker? With so much else to choose from, I don't think I'd have come out and paid $6 to hear a pseudo-Scot singing Victor Jara either. The whole of California is bursting with real Latin Americans after all! Probably the exotic music over here will prove to be British!

Oh well, it was still good to be there anyway, and to sing. Maybe I'll get back up again sometime: the person who was filling out the 'report' which they file on all performers, said how impressed she'd been. I hope she wasn't just being nice: it was hard going sometimes.

We covered the fare, just about.

I certainly feel much more confident about calling myself a musician now. Accepting the bad breaks, knowing that some days just don't go well, or your voice is off, or the guitar strings are damp and sticky. And that the show must go on no matter.

It always seemed somehow pretentious before.

I had hoped to clear a few hundred dollars though, to help with the car. It's vital to keep Yani working as a speaker just now, which is mostly expenses only. But she has bills to pay: especially the massive medical ones (but not only: phone, gas, water, clothes and shoes for Carlos . . .).

She's become quite a cult figure in the US resistance

*movement, and is constantly in demand. So she needs to
be independent. Anyway she's not fit enough yet to face
the demands of regular work, especially the labour of
cleaning or whatever, which seems most likely what's
available. The others have jobs, but I doubt they're well
paid . . . the rich lifestyle, which Californians seem to take
as their due, is largely kept afloat by 'illegal aliens'
working for peanuts to prime their gas pumps, clean their
houses, keep their sweatshops turning over . . .*

September 6th

*No trouble while I was away up north. But today, as
Carmen and I left for work just after 6 am (I drive her
down to catch a ride from a friend 5 or 6 miles south), we
spotted a strange van moving very slowly towards the
house. Well practised now, we drove on a block then
quickly doubled back. It had gone. But, rather than waiting
with her as usual, I came straight back. The van was
parked round behind the house. I try always to have a
camera in the car, and drove slowly past, taking pictures. I
hope they come out. I hope even more we don't need them
to.*

Later

*Checked again. The van is gone. It was pretty dirty—
like a jobbing builder's. But, almost the worst thing is that
you never know. We have to be especially on guard again
because Yanira spoke openly at an anti-death squad rally
on the steps of City Hall in downtown LA at the weekend.
She was televised—even if they didn't know before their
threats haven't worked, the bullies will know now. For
sure.*

At night the house feels very vulnerable: it has so many windows, and the curtains are very sketchy. Night comes early here—it's dark by 9 in the evening—and the street lights are very poor. The night is full of eyes.

September 30th

I'm really tired. I sleep on a couch close to the front door, just in case, and often things don't settle down till 12 midnight. Yani's meetings frequently keep her out later than this, and I have to be ready to let her in. (Some of her Salvadoran compas keep her close when she's out of the house.) Then down the road with Carmen at six.

In addition I'm working as a carpenter on the house itself more or less fulltime. (Frank and Elizabeth have turned out to be tremendous. They give us all kinds of support, and have slowed the work down for our sake, although they may lose financially if they don't get the house on the market soon. They bring roses from their own garden.)

But what's really got us on edge is that the phone threats have started up again, here even, with a number which is unlisted, and only given to very few people. Plus Yanira was followed again the other day, and by the same car which ran her and Carlito off the road that first time. And, to cap everything, the doctors are saying that it is virtually certain she won't be able to have any more children, her body has been too severely damaged.

How the hell have they got this number? And who gave it to them? The word is someone gave it away deliberately. What does that do the small circle of friends who are left?

In spite of all this the work goes on steadily. Almost

every member of the family seems to be involved in the
movement for justice, indirectly of course by supporting
Yani and keeping Carlito close, but also through the two
Salvadoran organisations they belong to: UMSL (Unión
de Mujeres Salvadoreñas Para La Liberación: Melida
Anaya Montes: Union of Salvadoran Women for the
Liberation: Melida Anaya Montes—Melida was killed in
the struggle) and MASPS (Movimiento Amplio de
Solidaridad con El Pueblo Salvadoreño: Broad Movement
in Solidarity with the People of El Salvador). These are
based in a church in downtown Los Angeles. They work—
so hard, on shoe string resources—to tell the US people
what's happening in El Salvador—especially the mayhem
the US government is causing there with its present
policies of support for the oligarchy and the status quo.
They ask the electorate here to get the administration to
change: to pull out that support, to leave the Salvadoran
people free to determine their own way, their own future.
Again the music has its place: one of the projects just now
is raising funds to bring Cutumay Camones up to the
States. Cutumay Camones is the FMLN's main musical
group, having much the same role that Victor and
Quilapayun and Inti Illimani had, first in Chile, and later
throughout the world: telling it like it is, moving people to
get involved, to change, to work. They have some
wonderful songs. There have been more demonstrations
against the death squads; against contra aid; speaking
tours up and down country for Yanira . . . a lot of work.

Plus one great thing: everyone came through back
home, and we have a new, little, secondhand car: duly
inconspicuous and reliable (we hope!). We paid $1,500.

October 1st

I don't believe it!!! An earthquake!! It whanged into Los

*Angeles this morning just as the little guys were getting
ready for school.*

October 3rd

*Well, we're all complete refugees now, living under
polythene in the back garden. We're not going back inside
for a week.*

*The shock was around 6.0 on the Richter scale. It felt
massive. The epicentre was close. Well, I've been
frightened before, but this . . . Who needs death squads?
And the aftershocks have been pretty scary too.*

*The little guys were just getting ready for school (about
7:30) and I was sitting playing the guitar, waiting to take
them down the road. They were upstairs, and this roaring,
rumbling sound: I thought they were dragging a bed across
the floor. But then the whole place started to shake!
Whooo! How can anything stand? I started to get up, but
it was impossible to move, the floor was heaving so. The
shock seemed to go on for ever—I'm just amazed
anything's still standing. Yet all we lost was one window-
pane—and that was already loose. Our house is 3 stories
high, tall for around here. But because it's timberframed it
flexed like a tree. Just a few blocks away several brick
buildings were completely wrecked.*

*As soon as the first shock was over, we tumbled out into
the garden, and sat in Yani's new car with the radio up full
blast. There is a plethora of local radio stations: news
came in quite fast: even the commercials were
interrupted—things must be serious! Major damage in
Whittier, where the epicentre struck. Bad news all over,
but not as bad as it might have been. Amazingly, given the
force, only a few people have been killed/injured.
Everyone came rushing home from work, and we spent*

the rest of the day setting up camp. Fortunately the rains have been holding off but nights are pretty wet, under the plastic especially, and wee Susanita, especially, is prone to chest troubles.

Poor Yanira is away in New York, on a speaking tour: she couldn't get through by phone for ages.

As far as the work on the house is concerned we're going ahead almost as if nothing had happened—keep off the high ladders for a while: that's about it!

The little ones are already playing 'terremotos': earthquakes, giggling away as they shake the seat I'm sitting on!

Women As Targets

A Conversation With Salvadoran Rape-Victim Yanira

Suddenly, I heard this voice say, "Don't try to move or turn around, or I'll kill you." They told me to get in the van. They put tape over my eyes. First...they asked me if I was with the FMLN, which I am not. I did not respond. They slapped me and said, "Well, we know you are." Another one of them said, "If you don't talk, we're going to make you talk." I didn't say anything...didn't even move. And then they said they were going to "make me feel good." They introduced this stick in my vagina...and at the same time they were hitting me. They said, "This time, we're going to make you talk." Then one of them said, "Let me see your hands," and he started cutting them. Another one of them lit a cigarette and put it to my hands, and then close to my vagina. They told me, "Do you remember that you have a child? Would you like to see us doing this to him?" I was thinking everything at the same time...about my son, my family...and I thought about all the people in El Salvador who have been killed who had been in the same situation as I was in [now]...

— Yanira, in an interview with KPFK's Nancy Clark

In that interview, Yanira described the night of July 7. In the month since then, more than 20 others have received death threats and reported being followed by suspicious cars or receiving crank telephone calls. Even as late as last week, members of refugee committees continued to report incidents like these to police. But the terror for Yanira actually began months before her abduction, as she relates in the following interview. A 24-year-old single mother, Yanira first came to this country in 1981, fleeing the worst of the death-squad terror in El Salvador. She began working in the solidarity movement here in Los Angeles in 1984. Though she talked with ease and was outwardly calm during the interview, one sensed the pain just beneath the surface. She fidgeted with her hands often pausing to rest one hand over her womb now and then, as if protecting herself.

WEEKLY: *We know that before you were kidnapped, there was another incident in which you were attacked by unknown assailants. Do you think that incident was also related to the alleged death squads here?*

YANIRA: It was a very strange and complicated thing. They got hold of me on Olive Street. They started beating me, but they didn't say a single word. I might have thought that it was just a common crime, but then again, they didn't rob me of anything. For a moment the thought passed through my mind that it could be related [to my political activity]. Afterward, I didn't think much of it, but a doubt still lingers...

WEEKLY: *Is it true that the men who kidnapped and tortured you told you that they were intentionally beginning with a woman, and that other women would follow?*

YANIRA: Yes. When they finished interrogating and beating me, they said among themselves, "Well, if this one doesn't talk, the others will." They said they knew who these other women were, "important ones" [in the solidarity movement], according to them. [They said they knew] when they were alone, where they lived.

WEEKLY: *Why do you think that they target women?*

YANIRA: They probably think that women are in a position to give them more information. It's that type of male thinking that makes the woman out to be weaker than men, that macho way of thinking.

WEEKLY: *How have Salvadoran women responded to this type of terror over the years?*

YANIRA: What it's done is given the woman more strength to continue her struggle. On many occasions [death-squad members] think that after [they attack], that women are going to distance themselves, but we have come to note that in most cases when they kill her child, or when the woman herself is raped, she picks up more strength to continue the struggle, so that this won't happen to other women.

WEEKLY: *Do you know other women who have suffered the same kind of torture that you were subjected to?*

YANIRA: I've met Marta Alicia [the Salvadoran woman who received the death list naming 19 local activists, and who had formerly been held prisoner and torured in El Salvador], and I've read a lot about other Salvadoran women who have gone through the same thing.

WEEKLY: *Is the way in which you were tortured similar to these other women?*

YANIRA: Yes. Identical, I would say.

WEEKLY: *Your son is 3½ years old. How conscious is he of what has happened?*

YANIRA: The first time I was attacked, he saw it all, because he was with me. He remained nervous afterward. When he saw me for the first time after I got out of the hospital, after the second attack, he asked me if that "bad man" had beaten me again. He still doesn't know about all that's happened; he thinks his mother has been sick. What's affected him is that he can't go out on the street to ride his bike like he used to, and his mother is not with him like before, when she used to take him to play in the park.

WEEKLY: *We've heard that your father, who lives in El Salvador, also received a threatening letter.*

YANIRA: It happened about two months ago. He told me he received a letter telling him to call me and tell me to stop my [political] activities, because if I didn't, something bad could happen to me. They said they knew what I was doing, and who my friends were.

WEEKLY: *How has all this affected your family? Do they want you to stop working in the solidarity movement?*

YANIRA: No, they haven't asked that of me; I don't know whether they've *thought* about it, but they haven't said anything. They're scared, of course, especially because my son has been threatened and there are other children in the family. But they feel that it's important to continue the struggle, because our struggle is a just one.

WEEKLY: *Your family agrees with your politics?*

YANIRA: Yes, my entire family.

WEEKLY: *Despite all that has happened, there are some people who still doubt that your case has a connection to the death squads in El Salvador. Harold Esell, the local Immigration Service chief, thinks it's a simple case of rape, not politically motivated.*

YANIRA: The people who doubt it are the same ones who don't recognize that there's a war going on in El Salvador, nor do they recognize the human rights violations that continue there. In the same way, even when we have 72,000 dead in El Salvador, they don't want to recognize what is happening here.

WEEKLY: *In the KPFK interview, you said that you were treated badly by the police officer who found you on the street, unconscious, after the kidnapping.*

YANIRA: After they [threw me out of the van], I waited awhile, thinking that they were going to come back any moment. Then I stood up and started to walk, but I fell because the pain was too great. Suddenly, I saw the flashlight in my face, and the policeman *ordered* me to give him my name and address, and [tell him] why I was there. In between the sobs and the pain, I began to tell him, but there was a moment in which he didn't understand me, and he said that if I didn't tell him my name and where I lived that he would leave me there. I just stared back at him, surprised at the way he was treating me. He was about to leave when the ambulance arrived.

WEEKLY: *Did you complain to the police about this officer's conduct?*

YANIRA: Yes, and according to [the police at the] Rampart station, they're trying to find out who it is. They haven't said anything to me yet.

WEEKLY: *Are you going to start working in solidarity again gradually, or all at once?*

YANIRA: It's definitely going to be all at once, starting maybe today or tomorrow. I would have liked to have done it sooner, but my physical health didn't allow me. But yes, I am going to continue working, the same as always. I think my work will be more consistent now, more committed.

WEEKLY: *Do the people who have helped you through this agree that you should start working again?*

YANIRA: Well, not really, because they're scared, and I think that it's generalized: We're *all* scared. All of us feel that it could happen again at any time. But if we didn't do it this way, we'd be letting them sow terror and allowing it to stop our work. And we're not going to let that happen.

—L.A. Weekly, August 14-20, 1987

5 For Those Who Die Singing

"Canto que has sido valiente: siempre sera canción nueva"

My song is not just for the singing
Nor to show off my voice
This song is for the guitar
Filled with feeling and wisdom

It has a heart of the earth
And the wings of a dove
It is like blessed water
Touching glories and sorrows with holiness
Thus is my song
Just as Violeta would have said
Hardworking guitar
Carrying the scent of spring

This guitar is not for the rich
How can it be?
My song is about the scaffolding—
Built to reach the stars
How deeply felt that song
Sung by one who will die singing
Truthfully singing his song

Passing flattery has no place
Nor worldwide fame
It is the song of this slender country

Springing from the very bones of its soil

Here, where everything ends
And everything begins
song forged in strength
Will always be new song

(Manifiesto: Victor Jara)

Killing Victor Jara was disgusting. It was also a bad
mistake. The killing spread his songs—with their poetry
and politics and passionate anger—to the whole world.

Back then, in 1973, outwith Chile how many people
knew about the destruction of Allende, of Victor, of the
thousands without name?

Contrast that with today: with the huge international
movement of resistance to the Central American war; the
thousands of US and European citizens living and working
in Nicaragua; the twinning of towns and hospitals and
schools and parishes between the North and El Salvador,
Guatemala, Nicaragua; the engineers, the teachers, the
mechanics and architects and farm workers and nuns, all
standing shoulder to shoulder with their friends facing
down their own government's mercenaries, draining back
into Honduras and Costa Rica.

Contrast that too with the growing awareness that there
is *one* war being waged: not just against the peoples of
Central and South America, but against the dispossessed
ones of the entire world. And that what they did to Victor,
and what they have done to Yanira, and to the thousands on
thousands of others, is just a horribly vicious way of doing
what daily hunger and lack of clean water do, little by little,
to millions on millions of innocent ones the world over,

every moment of every single day.

We know too that the war is not confined to the South: homelessness and unemployment; forced prostitution and inhuman work; consumerism and the destruction of the environment: all these are iron in the soul for those who cannot afford their appointed role as consumers, within the materialist North.

Our presentation before the Pope and the march on Balmoral welded justice irrevocably to peace. We began to see that all our apparently different causes were us tearing at the multiple masks of the one single monster. War; international injustice; under- and un-employment; the denial of human rights; the repression of women; the destruction of the world's natural resources; global pollution; the buying off and destabilising of democracy. All had their roots in the subordination of people to power; and within our supposed Christian society of caring love, to the making of the wealth which conveys that power.

Our courage was coming back: song and music were becoming strong within the movements once again. Songs from the peace camps; from the unemployed workers' marches; from the prisons and homelands of South Africa. Music's way of reaching across the barriers brought us together at a level which is impossible for straight speech.

Dazed by the successes of Bellahouston and Balmoral, I was tempted once again to abandon the guitar. To follow through fulltime—finding new ways to keep up the political pressure. But Victor. I was swept up into the beauty and tragedy of his story and captivated by the vivid courage and laughter of the Chileans.

They pointed us to Central America.

So much of our present awareness of the war there today is due directly to these exiles, borne to the four winds by that dreadful midwifery of the military.

This was the murderers' mistake. Their obscene brutality shocked many people into passionate action. No longer just

working for a cause, rather sharing life with their friends.
We were radicalised by what they gave us. The Nueva
Canción was far from destroyed in the brutality. It rapidly
became a movement, whose writers and singers built on
their own rediscovered culture to help develop the people's
spirit of resistance to foreign economic, political and, of
course, military, domination. Here were 'songs of revolution' with a vengeance: a music born in blood, sung not
from the safety of the wellpaid concert hall but from the
strikers' line under the police cannons, or echoing down the
mountains with the clattering rhythms of riflefire for
counterpoint. They were the songs of a family community
in struggle, sister laying down her life for brother, child for
father, mother for her children.

It was this fire, and the friendships forged in this fire,
which so thrilled us, forcefed for so long on statistics and
long distance ideals.

"Song which is forged in strength will always be new song"

"We have no chance of reclaiming Chile—yet," Sonia
said. "Look to Central America. Especially to Nicaragua.
There the tide of intervention has been stopped—for the
moment. The Sandinistas are like Dr. Allende in our
country, returning to the people their labour and their land.
But again the vultures of the CIA are gathering to wreck
their work, as they did ours in 1973. Join Nicaragua now,
maybe we can turn that tide back on itself. And then, one
day, we'll all go back to Chile, singing."

Anne, a co-worker at SEAD, handed me a letter. It told of
a journey for peace and self-determination through Central
America. The plan originated with a Norwegian group,
which had been working particularly against weapons pro-
liferation. It was especially attractive because they too were
now trying to make the links between war and dis-

possession. They had plenty of experience organising massive marches and rallies, and they had connections— with human rights groups, with unions and churches and political parties—in each of the countries of the region. The co-ordinating committee had representatives from as many of the participating countries as possible, and march organisers had been working in Central America for the past year.

'La Marcha por la Paz' was planned for December 1985 and January 1986. For me it was the perfect link between Bellahouston, Puerto Montt and Nicaragua.

And it was to bring me here, in the end.

We met up just outside Panama city. Three hundred of us from 25 countries. From colleges, unions, churches, political parties, solidarity groups, peace camps, religious orders. People came from as far away as Australia and India, and from as close as California and Texas. Most of us could speak only a smattering of Spanish, and few had been in Latin America before. Our goals were simple, to show the people of Nicaragua and El Salvador and the rest that there were many thousands angry at the war being forced on them by our societies; that we knew how they were suffering and wanted to be with them; and that we would support them in their struggle to take their own lands back from the oligarchies and the multinationals—and our own demands for cheap coffee and beef.

In each of the seven countries we would be passing through, committees had been established, again drawn from the same range of organisations as the 'marchistas' themselves. Each was working out a programme of 7 days, more or less: meetings with local communities, cultural events, visits to politicians, church leaders, co-operatives, unions. The ominous exceptions were Guatemala and El Salvador. In these—both claimed by the US to be democracies, in distinction from 'communist' Nicaragua of course—it was extremely difficult for such events to be organised. Too many people had already disappeared. The Guatemalan committee had to work from exile, they were in such danger.

It's hard to know where to begin or what to leave out. Panama was really peculiar. Dominated by the US—its main currency even being the US dollar: it was the principal banking centre for the whole Caribbean. Howard airbase— from which the tentacles of US airpower stretched over the whole of Central America—was just outside Panama city. The very country was cut in two by the Panama Canal, controlled by the US.

General Omar Torrijos was the hero of the time: somehow he had managed to negotiate a treaty with the US which ceded the canal zone back to Panama at the end of 1999. We went to his tomb—his plane had exploded in mysterious circumstances—we were given Torrijos posters and T-shirts. At the same time we heard how the treaty had a great deal of small print: the US keeping the right to maintain airbases in Panama, the right to challenge any tariffs which they felt to be 'unreasonable,' and so, innocently no doubt(!), on.

Panama wasn't strictly speaking Central America—it had been artificially created at the turn of the century, when the US had 'encouraged' local separatist movements on the isthmus to break away from the rest of Columbia. Together with Mexico, again part of the main continent to the north (especially if the US were to return to it the lands which had been abrogated and settled as California, Texas, Arizona, New Mexico), it had been chosen as a pole for the march because of its role in working for peace in Central America. Mexico, Panama, Venezuela and Columbia together comprised the 'Contadora' group, so named from the island where they met to hammer out a peace plan for the region. On the advice of the Central Americans themselves we took, as themes for the march, the main proposals of this group of countries: the full observance of the United Nations' code of human rights; and 'autodeterminación': the removal of foreign troops from the region, the right to hold unmolested elections, the stopping of all undue pressure through bribes, threats, economic and other embargoes.

It made for nice symbolism to begin in the one, Panama, and to end in the other, Mexico. It made for probable trouble that the U.S. had constantly been subverting Contadora, claiming the whole of Central America as its backyard.

The first part of the journey looked straightforward. We left Panama city in a huge convoy of buses, heading north, calling at several small towns en route. It was horribly sticky; mosquitoes bit us to bits; the crickets filled the night with their constant shrilling. It had been a major task to find places suitable for such a large group of people— softish Northerners especially—we camped in schools, on college campuses, on the bare ground. My abiding memories of Panama are: such slums, and such wealth, as we were to see nowhere else; the towering banks; the obscene power of the planes of war; a US holiday cruise ship sidling through the canal, a few yards and a whole world away from the impoverished Panamanians themselves.

And Emilio and Fernando and myself, from different sides of that one world, unable to converse in either Spanish or English, finding our common language singing Victor's songs under the stars.

Those and my first encounter with the death squads.

'Costa Rica Libre'—'Free Costa Rica'—was an ultra rightwing group, part of the network of such organisations found in all the 'democracies' of which the US presidents are so proud. As we approached the border between Panama and Costa Rica we heard that Costa Rica Libre was waiting for us just across the fence. They were armed: with knives, and guns, and chains, and their declared purpose was to prevent us leaving Panama.

The Costa Rican press was already mounting a campaign against the march: calling us communists (what else? The trick of course is leftover McCarthyism: keep quiet: so you *are* a communist—'silence is consent'; deny: Aha, you agree: Communism *is* evil. In the real world of repression and starvation, christians and communists often find common ground—the work for justice). But, since Costa Rica was held up as the quintessential democracy of Central America, we felt that, even so, there would be no real problem getting in. How wrong we were!

We blundered into the customs compound between the two countries in the middle of the night. We were still acclimatising, short of sleep, riddled with diarrhea. Just outside was a bar, pulsating with garish lights and loud music. Very loud.

The buses dumped us out into the clamorous darkness, turned tail and disappeared. We numbly organised a patrol to walk the fence round through what was left of the night, and settled down to try to sleep. Between the racket from the cantina, the huge trucks rolling into the compound to wait for clearance in the morning, and the knowledge that Costa Rica Libre were just the other side of the wire, sleep came reluctantly.

With the dawn we saw just how bleak our situation was. The compound was flat concrete, surrounded by a 10 foot high wire mesh fence, with a storage shed in the centre. It had one tap of impure water, no shops and no toilets.

A series of shocks rolled in on us: first, the buses which we'd engaged to meet us here and to take us all the way on to Mexico were 'no longer available' (The company had been threatened with reprisals if they carried us 'communistas'); next, the Costa Rican government 'could no longer guarantee our security'; and, lastly (for the moment), our permission to travel through Costa Rica was revoked 'for our own safety.'

Under a withering sun, we negotiated desperately throughout the day. There was little shade, the concrete hummed with heat. Time and again we'd form ourselves into lines, bags repacked, expecting new buses to appear, and the journey to continue. One moment we'd be going back, another going on. The march had tried to establish a democratic structure right from the start. But, with so many people from so many different countries, taking part for such a variety of reasons, it had proved really hard to work. Consensus needs time. And time, with every comment or statement or question having to be translated either into Spanish or into English, with 300 people to engage somehow, and with Costa Rica Libre pounding up and down just a few yards away, we simply did not have.

In the circumstances, it's surprising this first real test was met as well as it was. As ever, a handful of people emerged with great practical nous. We were suspended in no man's land. Once inside the compound we were unable to leave it again: our Panamanian supporters set up a food line; the mysterious packages which had been carried all the way from Europe were broken open, and proved (thankfully!) to be field toilets; the bright banners, made for demonstrations, were quickly adapted, becoming screens to preserve our modesty; water purifying tablets became the new gold.

After the sweltering heat, torrential rain. Nowhere to keep dry, sleeping bags and clothes saturated. Still no news of any sort of breakthrough. Benjamino Pisa, the Costa Rican minister of security, came to meet with the march leaders. He was "very sorry" about the trouble, but repeated that our safety could not be guaranteed; and since, coincidentally no doubt, the buses had abandoned us, urged us strongly to go back to Panama city.

It just happened that Pisa was a founder member of Costa Rica Libre.

Negotiations dragged on way into the second night. We were adamant: we were *not* going back. Apart from that killing the march off almost before it had begun, we had already imposed ourselves on our Panamanian hosts for long enough. They had coped with the logistics of feeding, housing and transporting 300 disoriented gringos admirably for almost two weeks now. They did not need us flooding back in defeat.

A compromise: Pisa would give us a three day transit visa provided we refrained from any political activity, and went directly from the border to the capital: San José. And from San José directly to Nicaragua, way to the North. This was his last offer. Sadly it meant abandoning all the communities along our route who had planned receptions for us, but it was either this, or it was back home.

On our acceptance of these terms, the gates suddenly opened up, all customs examinations were waived, and buses magically rematerialised.

No one in the camp was content with the outcome, but the Canadian contingent was outraged. They came from years of peace action, and were very strong on non-violent resistance. They were *not* going to be carted off ignominiously, mob or no mob. The rest of us could go on if we wanted to; they would wait till we'd gone, then, banners flying, they would walk across the border into Costa Rica, and, if necessary, into the weapons of the expectant fascisti.

We pleaded with them in vain. Until I'd met the Chileans, and heard what apartheid had done to Nelson Mandela and the others who had tried for so long to hold to the nonviolent way, I'd also felt that such pacifism was the way forward, in every circumstance. For doesn't violence inevitably beget violence? And aren't *all* our revolutions always 'for the better?' I could no longer be so sure. Even

Gandhi chose his points of resistance very carefully. Most of us felt that this was not the moment for heroics—we knew too little of the ways of the place, and too many people, who had worked so hard, were expecting us.

In another teeming downpour we piled onto the buses, sloshing through the pouring drains. The 20 or so Canadians, plus a dozen supporters from other countries, sat singing in a circle, tears streaming down their cheeks. Many people on the buses were crying as well. After a maudlin eternity the engines started up, and we pulled slowly through the gates, leaving them to the rain and to Costa Rica Libre.

We made about 100 yards. Then, inexplicably, the buses were halted, pulled over. Police and soldiers appeared on every side, and the interminable negotiations began again. The sun burst out and began to incinerate us. It appeared that we did need to go through the customs formalities after all. Surprise! Another sweltering wait of several hours; finally our passports reappeared and were lethargically disbursed. We were given transit visas, just 72 hours to cross Costa Rica from Panama to Nicaragua.

Just as the buses were beginning to move again, the Canadians arrived, panting up the road in our wake. Other marchers had used the new holdup to go back and had finally talked them into coming with us.

This incident woke us up to the potentially explosive differences of cultures that we were mixing, and we resolved to follow the advice of the local support groups in future, when such differences arose.

It was close: the march could easily have fallen apart if our dissidents had actually been abandoned.

Costa Rica is celebrated for having no army. Well, we were locked into the buses, with a soldier posted at both doors. They wore the standard fatigues, helmets and boots, they carried automatic rifles and teargas canisters. The march met their exact replicas in Honduras, El Salvador and Guatemala: definitively army—made in the USA, whatever the propaganda said. They guarded us all the way to San José. The only drinks we had were what we carried in our bottles, the foul mixture of bad water and chlorine tablets. Diarrhea was still rampant. We had no food. It took 12 hours. They allowed us off the buses once only, very early on, to relieve ourselves at the roadside. After that, although they stopped often to drink and for the toilet, we were prevented from so much as stretching our legs.

The horrible journey was nothing compared with what was waiting for us in San José. As we drew up before the hostel where we were to stay, Costa Rica Libre, again most mysteriously, materialised. Rocks crashed against the buses, chants and obscenities fell on us like spit. A thin line of security police forced a narrow corridor through for us, and, heads down, muffled up against the missiles, we made a run for the building. There was no sanctuary, the windows caved in, tear gas bursting.

The Costa Rican support groups, waiting ever since the bad news from the border, quickly organised makeshift defences: turning planks and tables against the windows as barricades, and forming a patrol to keep anyone from rushing the front. Ominously, we found they'd stacked crudely made clubs behind the doors, ready to repel the final assault. They suffered several casualties: one man lost an eye, and several little children were caught by an exploding teargas canister. (We found one later: it was standard US issue. Some were even thrown by the security forces, not the rioters.)

I've never been so frightened—well, until this last, even closer, encounter with the murderers—someone would certainly be killed before the night was over. A young Costa Rican climbed up in front of us and, with huge black eyes, cried out a welcome against the horrible pandemonium. Calmly she gave us the practical arrangements, raising a great cheer when she announced that the food was ready, and that, mob or no mob, *she* was hungry anyway. Her example was the more infectious in that the corners of her smile were trembling slightly. We started singing, and, as the queues formed up as best they could under the barrage, I sat and played to help calm things down.

It was a long night. After more than 2 hours the riot suddenly switched off like a light. No charges were made to clear the street, no sudden cavalry forces came thundering to our rescue: it was obvious someone had given a signal: hold off for the moment. Our suspicions grew when Pisa immediately sent a message that, since we had 'engaged in political activity,' even the limited visas he had allowed so reluctantly were cancelled. Once again he could no longer guarantee our security (it had been *guaranteed* so far!?), and, unless we left, at once, he could not be responsible for what might happen. All this at 3 am, on top of that dreadful journey, the lack of sleep and the riot.

We dug in: there were the children, the man who'd lost his eye, there were several marchers already sick, getting worse by the minute. Everyone had to rest, we said, and we wanted time for the doctors to do their work. "No." Pisa set a deadline for 6 am, after which his forces would be withdrawn and the marchers left to the mob.

The hours till the deadline were strange. The sun rose on the shattered hostel, with people strewn all over the site, still fully dressed, trying to rest behind whatever defences they could find. Across the narrow street lounged the soldiers—they'd moved Costa Rica Libre up about 100 yards (they were still—too!—clearly audible)—and were holding the road in front of the hostel as a no go area. On our front lawn were a variety of religious people, Christians reading bibles; Buddhist monks chanting and sounding prayer drums; others meditating silently. We wanted to let people see for themselves the variety of the marchers' beliefs, over against the 'communist' gibes. Behind the soldiers the advance guard of our developed civilisation, Colonel Sanders of fried chicken infamy, smirked fatuously from a shop front.

The sense of unreality was heightened when the 'periodistas'—journalists—straggled out into the eerily empty space between the fence and the soldiers. We formed a line to call home from a public phone, on the street corner. I had a letter from Nelson Gray of Scottish Television. I used it to join them. Stepping down onto that road was very strange: dreamlike, somehow out of time. Would we get across the road? Somehow round the soldiers, suggestively peeling oranges with their huge knives? To stand numbly, waiting on connections. At last to speak to Marion sitting thousands of miles away in the SEAD office. Suspended in that limbo between worlds, we called Australia and India and Scotland and New York. Carefully, we stepped jerkily back to the gates, shoulders stiff against the malign presence behind us.

The deadline came. And went. The soldiers lounged on; the screams and catcalls and whistles showed no sign of dying out.

Another deadline was set. Again it came. And went.

Reluctantly we loaded the buses in the late morning. Leaving was terrible. The Costa Rican families who had welcomed us, and stayed through that awful night with us, formed a singing, clapping corridor and, slowly we wound our way through them, catching hands, embracing, kissing...We were all in tears, and everyone was saying: "Come back soon: please: Most Costa Ricans are not like these fascistas—all we want is peace" (how that single wistful refrain haunted us throughout Central America: "All we want is peace"). The worst of it was the uncertainty we were bequeathing them: anyone who left the grounds of the hostel had to pass the security block—and give their names. They had taken huge risks in coming into the open to welcome the march, hoping our presence would provide security for letting the world see the clandestine militari-sation of Costa Rica. And already we were leaving, their hopes in shreds, and Costa Rica Libre on the rampage.

One thing, the march had a video crew travelling with it; and they had taken footage of the riot, from start to finish. The local CBS people suddenly appeared, offering to buy the film, begging for it. The big news was nothing to do with the children who had been hurt, or the person who'd been blinded, or the forgotten war. It was that the march included 100 North Americans; on the receiving end of such violence. They were excited, promising to wire it up to the US at once, for nationwide transmission. We handed it over. Costa Rican TV also covered the riot. Later, in Nica-ragua, we heard that Pisa had been demoted for his part in the affair, partly thanks to the outrage triggered by that coverage; and that one of the second rank presidential candidates, Oscar Arias Sanchez, had taken up our watch-words of peace through self-determination, and was moving ahead. (His bid was successful, and, as president, he received the Nobel Prize in 1987 for his Central American peace plan.)

Our footage? When we got to the States we found that it had never been shown.

What happened? An inefficient transfer service, although we'd given it into CBS's own hands? Or control of the 'free media' by the interests which would have whipped such an outrage into cause for invasion—if it had happened in Nicaragua?

We had to run the gauntlet again: heads down, shields at the windows we roared through the mob. Lights and windows shattered, rocks rattled off the roof. Once more locked into the buses; once again soldiers taunting us as they stopped to buy drinks and to use the restrooms; once again the stifling heat and the endlessly churning stomachs.

Twelve hours later we were in Nicaragua.

Thanks to Costa Rica Libre we were now several days ahead of schedule. Despite this the Nicaraguan buses were there waiting at the border crossing at Peñas Blancas. For all that it was the middle of the night, the whole welcoming group was there, filling the night with smiles and music.

We were rushed to a school campus, for a welcoming ceremony (gratefully cut down to suit the time), food was magically conjured out of the darkness, and we collapsed into deep sleep at last.

To sing the song of Nicaragua would take endless books.

We knew how the people had risen against the appalling dictator, Somoza, corrupt grandson of the US appointee who had had General Sandino murdered. We knew how the country had organised itself since the revolution, living out Sandino's dream of self-determination. How high school students had poured into the countryside to bring the harvests home *and* to teach everyone to read and write. We had seen the World Health Organisation's careful documentation of the eradication of the supposedly endemic diseases of malaria and tuberculosis as the people carried through a comprehensive vaccination programme. We knew how the land was being given back to those whose centuries of blood had kept the fruit and coffee company profits high.

We knew that the North had installed the grandfather and supported the grandson up till the very last moment, and that it was now doing everything it could to reverse the revolution. Unable to endure such 'communism' (for all its roots in the Bible and the Liberty Bell), the US had mined Nicaragua's harbours, against international law. It was overflying the country, against international law. It was paying and supplying a proxy mercenary army, based in Honduras and Costa Rica, but with the elected government of Nicaragua as its target, against international law. Just as

Somoza had done, this army—the 'contras'—was waging a war of terrorism against the ordinary men and women of the farms and plantations: children were being killed, hospitals sabotaged, buses blown to bits. We knew that the US, having imposed its own economic blockade against the tiny country, was fiercely pressuring other nations to follow suit (and that Britain, almost alone, was supportive of the US position).

All this we knew: *not* from the Nicaraguan government, but from a whole range of people and organisations across the world who had worked and lived in Nicaragua. They had no special axes to grind, no 'backyard' to exploit. Their job was to report the real facts of any conflict, to work to stop torture, ensure that children get fed, set prisoners free.

We had not known the faces of the mothers of the young men, and women, flung to the fighting: their anguish and pride as they told their stories. What we had not seen were the shattered remains of the little farms, wrecked with savagery beyond belief. We knew nothing of the graves scattered along the roadside, the church walls pitted with machine gun holes, the whole villages mourning the toddlers mown down by the machine guns our dollars and pounds had provided.

We had not yet seen the children dancing, nor caught the quiet determination as the people picked through the rubble to start, once again, to rebuild. We had not yet seen the Sandinista commandantes sitting patiently for hours under the sun, surrounded by the ordinary people: listening to their needs and complaints, explaining why this was being done, or that; or, even more astonishing to those of us who had tried to talk into the deaf ear of our controlled democracy, to hear them saying: 'Yes, we were wrong. We're sorry, tell us what we should do here.'

Nor had we yet sat with some of the few people who had actually voted communist in Nicaragua, and heard them openly accusing the Sandinistas of being too capitalist! We had not yet heard politicians from every party acknowledging the elections as fair.

Above all we had not yet caught that wonderful spirit of independence and personal worth, which saw a tiny country of 3 million, taking on this overwhelming power, knowing that, in the end, the monster had no spirit and was already defeated.

We came to the southern town of Rivas.

There was a tremendous rally through the streets, and Padre Ernesto Cardenal, one of the four famously turbulent priests of the Nicaraguan government, met us. He spoke, movingly, simply, poet as he is, in the town square. I was proud to be on the platform with him, under the Nicaraguan flag.

I left the buses briefly to take in Belén, just below Rivas, where a medical centre was being rebuilt, with support from Scottish people. Mike and Nick, who were part of the medical team, greeted me with their sharp Scottish humour: told how the original tiny centre had to serve some 24,000 people; how the new building would more than double the effectiveness of their work. How the imposed war was wrecking so much that the people had achieved, in health, in education, in freedom. How the National Guard had come in the last throes of Somoza's reign of terror, pretending to be guerrillas. They massacred those who came to greet them, and flung their bodies into the drinking water well of the centre. The people filled the well in, raising over it a simple monument to their dead ones.

Mike had married a Nicaraguan.

On up to Managua, for a major rally, downtown, in La Plaza de la Revolución. Another priest, the Foreign Minister, Miguel d'Escoto, spoke. Afterwards he came to the university where we were camped, for a long session of questions and open discussion. Again we were struck with his gentleness and readiness to try genuinely to answer, whatever the question. It was in Managua, too, that we attended the 'cara al pueblo,' when all the commandantes came together to respond to questions, undefended in front of all the people and the unwinking eyes of the television cameras.

Also impressive in all of this, was the nearly non-existent security. On stage with Miguel d'Escoto or Padre Ernesto, children were running free, dogs coming and going, any number of photographers. At the cara al pueblo, everyone just piled in, so close that people in the front rows had simply to reach out to touch President Ortega. It said so much for the genuineness of the Sandinistas' claims that they were truly representing the people, that they could be so open, taking risks none of our politicians would dream of allowing their precious selves. There were plenty of guns around; this was a country at war. But what was remarkable was the absence of fear, of defensiveness, between the leaders and their people. This was obvious not only in the casual security but also in the soldiers and people inter-mingling freely, with weapons laid calmly on café tables, and even passed from hand to hand. All in total contrast to what we saw in the other Central American states, where relations were at best something like our own, with the soldiers strictly forbidden from 'fraternising' with their own people, and, at worst, where they drove around in high trucks with their guns trained on the people in the street below them.

And since the collapse of our puppet, Somoza, there have been no death squads in Nicaragua.

After Managua we headed north, up into the mountains and contra country, above Esteli.

Journal at the Frontline 6

October 14th

We reclaimed the house from the grumbling ground about a week ago. Just in time—the first of the autumn rains came on pellmell, drilling holes into the dust.

First night back inside, Antonio was away, so Carmen slept downstairs with their little ones.

As usual I was tucked discreetly away in my nook by the front door.

God knows when it was, but suddenly, in the blackest night, Carmen started screaming and screaming and screaming. Torn from my sofa by the sheer intensity of the noise, I stumbled through: still more than half asleep, the murderers had come back at last. But she was alone, sitting bolt upright between the two little ones, lying one on either side. What? Where? Nobody else was moving. The house seemed solid. Had there been another earthquake? How had I slept through it? Was everyone else dead?

The hair is still pricking at the back of my neck. That unearthly screaming, on and on, in the dark brooding house.

Holding Carmen's hand, in the end she managed to tell me: in one of the passageways leading off the room, she had glimpsed a dark silhouette: a man. But who? And where was he now? She's hallucinating, I thought—we've all been living on our nerves for months now. But . . .gripping my hand so tightly, she was so sure . . .Maybe we were haunted . . .

I grabbed some clothes, and a torch, and opened the back door up to let Ranger out (it wasn't locked: Carmen was saying she'd heard it bang shut). Ranger's old and tired: he hadn't even roused at the racket, but now, thinking we were going for a midnight cat hunt, he went rushing out into the dark, ferreting eagerly this way and that. Nothing. I went out after him, cautiously, sidling along the wall of the house. Pale, pale light, with huge chasms of deep shadow. Nobody. Wait—that rustling! Just the dog scruffling about in the leaves behind the garage. He came trotting up, eyes bright in the torchlight, tongue lolling: nothing to report.

Joanna, Carmen's other sister, appeared. We made a round of all the rooms, checking that everyone was OK. We three were the only ones awake, even Ranger had had enough and was settling back to sleep.

We laughed about it all, in the morning. Especially because I'd been sleeping under just a sheet, wearing nothing. I took that sheet with me to meet the contras, clutched in front, but when I turned away from Carmen to get my clothes . . .!!

Someone had been there, he'd dropped a cigarette butt just where Carmen had said, while the backdoor had banged shut: presumably as he hurtled off up the road!

My heart is still pounding—he must still be running!

What else can happen, for goodness sake? I'm going back to Scotland!

November 3rd

What else can happen?—another bad question.

This very morning we got a confused phone call from a family uncle. He heard on the news something about Yanira, who's away on a speaking tour. "Take care of Carlos," he kept saying, over and again. The news seems to have been saying: "Yanira, do you know where your son is now?"

But that's crazy: news programmes don't carry that sort of message. Do they?

Later

Nothing more, although we've been trying to monitor the radio. Can't reach Yanira either.

November 5th

Yani called yesterday.

Apparently what's happened is that the group who was sponsoring her speaking in the East found a flyer advertising the meeting thrust back under their door. It had a crude drawing of Carlito scrawled on it—with his head torn off. And: "Where is your son right now, bitch? This is what we're going to do to him."

She sounded shaken, but the tour is going ahead.

Also, last week, they slaughtered Herbert Anaya Sanabria, Director of the Human Rights Office in San Salvador. They cut him down in front of his wife and children.

The phones are ringing again: threats to La Señora

*Sanabria and all her five children. Unspeakable mouthings
about Carlos and Yanira.*

*What have they done, for heaven's sake? Dared to
dream; dared to try to make that dream reality. The dream
of Martin Luther King, and Archbishop Oscar Romero:
food, water, education, housing, health for all.*

The dream that makes us all "Filthy Communists!!"

What did the children ever do, for God's sake?!

*"That every child may one day have a lunch box?
with food to put inside it, day on day?*

*That every child may have a school
to bring that lunchbox to?"*

A simple dream indeed.

*Why are we so frightened of it? And why is it crushed
down so brutally?*

6 Ay Nicaragua, Nicaraguita

"The contras will never win—they have no good songs!"

(Carlos Mejia Godoy)

Mr. Reagan gave the order
Said we're not to cross this border

Yet we're 5,000 miles away from home

Why did we ever come?—
We're missing Christmas home with Mum

And we're 5,000 miles away from home

We've been gassed and we've been stoned
And we're weary to the bone

And we're 5,000 miles away from home

From Scotland to Japan
We don't want another Vietnam

That's why we're 5,000 miles away from home

Sandino's at our side
You GIs you'd better hide

When we're 5,000 miles away from home

Nicaragua will stay free:
To hell with Ron and Mrs. T

That's why we're 5,000 miles away from home

(Border song: adapted from Woody Guthrie's "500 miles")

The mountains around Esteli are very beautiful. How can they bear such bitter fruit? The war has raged over them for almost a decade now: Somoza's collapse began here, in bitter fighting, and here the contras from Honduras creep down to savage the farms and the schools.

Here, above all, the children: 'Santos inocentes'—Holy Innocents: wallposters all over town of the 4 year olds the contras had slaughtered: a whole school dancing and singing and laughing with us. Here the little ones holding placards mutely as the buses pulled out: "Queremos Paz Solamente—All we want is peace": "Los niños quieren vivir en paz—we children just want to live in peace." That same message.

Everywhere we were struck by the political awareness of the ordinary people. Most had never even been down to Managua, a couple of hundred miles to the south. For them, the coffee, the land, the multinationals, the revolution are life and death—when for us, so often, these are 'issues' to take up or drop depending on our energy or because we might not like the coffee's taste.

In Nicaragua, and throughout that world we have designated 'Third,' no matter what the fashion, the children are still standing, mutely holding their signs. And the children still dance.

We spent Christmas in Esteli. A huge religious explosion in supposedly atheist dominated Nicaragua. On Christmas night we went with everyone else in the town to the

large church, which held court in the main square. It was
packed; the few people in uniform present formed part of
the congregation. The fervour was intense, the singing
raucous and completely uninhibited. There was certainly no
evidence of religious repression.

Back to the camp, and bed. As we were floating off to
sleep, the whole place blew up: machine guns ripping the
silence to shreds, windows blazing with incandescent flares,
tracers searing across the night sky. The contras, caught up
with us at last?

No: just the wicked 'communist' soldiers celebrating
Christmas!

Our last camp in Nicaragua was up above Esteli, at El
Espino, to the north of Somoto. To make the independent
nature of the march clear, we said goodbye to all our Nicaraguan friends in Somoto and headed on into the border
hills alone. The Pan-American highway, on which so much
of our travelling had been done, was narrow here, and the
hills seemed to crowd us closer. The entire 300 moved up in
a block. A hundred yards back from the actual crossing
point, we held a reclaiming ceremony in the shattered ruins
of what had once been the border post. The contras had
torched it, leaving a twisted filigree of metal framing,
seeded with shrapnel and pulverised glass. We read poems
and sang and kept silent for the friends we had made and
the friends we had already lost before knowing them.

A few people went on up to the border itself, and came
back with disturbing news. The Honduran side was buzzing
with soldiers and military vehicles, and the word was we
would not be allowed across. More sinister yet, the normal
border guards had been reinforced with the 'Cobras,' a
specialy trained crack unit who specialised in 'keeping the
peace,' brutally.

During the night we heard occasional gunfire, and were

grateful for the small detachment of Sandinista troops camped close by. Early next day official word from Honduras: 'The soldiers have orders to stop you crossing the border. They will shoot if necessary.'

Four on four we began to walk the last distance. Under pressure our organisation had developed considerably: veterans from the peace campaigns had shared their skills in non-violent resistance, and instructions were passing down the line: When the teargas starts, keep low: have a handkerchief ready wetted to hold over your mouth and nose: crawl away from the centre of the fumes: link up: hold on to the person next to you until you can see clearly again: if they grab you, go limp: if they start shooting, lie flat and try to roll off the road into the ditch.

Teargas? Shooting? For what?

After San José we knew that this was no game, and, with real fear, cold under the rising sun, we inched our way forward. Around the corner we came, the banners of the great dream floating over our heads: 'Selfdetermination,' 'All We Want Is Peace,' 'Viva Nicaragua, Honduras Y Escocia': the monks' prayer drums beating, the chants ringing: masked and helmeted soldiers clamped right across the road, machine guns, grenades and teargas canisters at the ready.

As we appeared they tensed, tightening their line, shifting their grips on the guns. Right on up we went, the drums marking our steps in the clear light, the shadows pacing doggedly beside us. Just short of the line we stopped, just before they unleashed the teargas, and in a single rippling, the entire length of the crowd sat down in the road.

There they stood and there we sat for the long, long day. Negotiators went back and forth, rumour countermarched with rumour: the soldiers were going to rush us; they were going to give way; we were going to stay there all night; we were coming back in the morning; the US consul in

Honduras was there behind the lines in person; the contras were gathering in the hills to attack us during the night.

The hard facts remained the faceless masks, the unyielding line, the burning sun.

The Nicaraguans advised us to pull back to the campground for the night: it would be too dangerous up at El Espino, and they could not provide enough troops to guard us. Everyone wanted to sit it out, but again we accepted guidance and went reluctantly back. We decided two things: a group to dash back to Managua, fly into Tegucigalpa, the Honduran capital, and link up there with the march support groups coming down to the border from the north. The rest would wait it out.

So the next 5 days. Each morning we cleared up camp, ready just in case for the crossing, and each evening we unpacked again, wearily, for another night. The buses ran us up, decanted us and retired to Somoto. The food was put together by the most enterprising national group of the whole march: the Spaniards. Led by a huge piratical man, Paco, they had somehow acquired an ancient jalopy—not to mention the precious petrol to run it—and went on forays into Somoto and the villages round. There they managed to concoct delicious meals of rice and chicken and beans (frijoles), salad and coffee, using the kitchens of some friends they had cultivated in a local hotel. The whole enterprise had a delightfully undercover tang to it, and, with the army water truck which came by every other day plus yet more field toilets, we were well enough provided with the basics. For the rest, one of the buses ran down into Somoto from time to time, to the market, to the ever-extending phone line, to the one cafe.

The delegation got into Honduras by air, and started to make its way down to meet us across the border. By the second day we had organised ourselves into orderly patterns: a few people stayed back in the camp, Paco and Co. set off on the day's foraging, the march co-ordinators and the day's crop of journalists went down into Somoto, the remainder of us sat it out on the road. Since we were refusing to leave, the Honduran authorities had closed the crossing completely, except for local people on foot. So we used the space between the soldiers and ourselves as an impromptu stage, with presentations made by the different national groups through the day. There was plenty of song and even laughter, juggling and miming. (It was in this crucible that the immortal poetry at the head of the chapter was born.) We tried everything we knew to reach out to the soldiers: even the onetime novice singing Gregorian chant. And indeed, gradually, the tension eased. One day the masks were gone, another the thick hedge of men had thinned, a third we even caught some of them grinning at particularly crazy antics.

> "From Scotland to Japan
> We don't want another Vietnam
> That's why we're 5,000 miles away from home"

One morning we arrived and began to squat down as usual: word jumped down the line: "Don't sit down, whatever you do!" Up ahead people were scratching themselves as if tearing their skins off. There were seed pods scattered all across the road, shedding tiny prickles which, once embedded, set up terrible irritation. It was a nice touch: non-violent action by the soldiers. The seed was known as 'pica-pica.'

Next day some of the US delegates performed a new dance: the 'Pica-Pica,' filled with dervish-like scratching: it had the soldiers really laughing.

Once we'd laughed together the tension was never the same. But whatever about the dancing and the laughter, the border was still adamantly closed. It was quite clear that the guards were under orders from some higher command that we were simply not to be allowed through—no matter what. Blase Bonpane, Director of Office of the Americas (Santa Monica, California), one of the march leaders, was summoned over to the Honduran immigration offices (ironically painted on their side: "Bienvenido a Honduras: Welcome to Honduras!") There he was confronted by a mysterious (US?) official dressed in a white tropical outfit: 'You will *not* be allowed through, no matter how long you stay here,' he was told. 'Go back to Managua and overfly this country altogether.'

Word came through that our 5th column had been stopped on the road down to El Espino, and turned back to Tegucigalpa. So on the 6th day, feeling we had shown how closed the US's Honduran democracy really was, and to get ready for El Salvador, we packed up and rode back to Managua.

The Sandinistas said: "Our people need their buses back, the university you stayed in is back on campus, we have our own work to do. You're welcome to stay longer, but you're on your own: go wherever you want, see whatever you want."

We did: some people went back upcountry to work on the coffee; others went to the beach to relax; a contingent flew across to the Atlantic coast to talk with the Miskito people, whose enforced resettlement early on was constantly used to blacken the revolution throughout the world (despite the Sandinistas' open admission of the wrongness of some of their actions). Still others set up more meetings: with opposition parties, with the real Communists, with women's groups.

The contrast between this openness and our treatment in the 'fledgling democracies' hardly needs to be noted.

I went to the British Embassy to get help with meeting Cardinal Obando y Bravo. This man, head of the Roman Catholic church, had angered people throughout the world by celebrating his first mass as cardinal in the Americas, not in Nicaragua with his wartorn people, but up in Miami, with contra leaders in the congregation. People back home wanted me to ask him about this. We wanted to tell him of our experiences throughout the country: the churches full, the people free. I was carrying a book of testimonies, independently gathered and carefully corroborated, telling at first hand the sufferings endured by unarmed civilians at the hands of the contras. Collated by Teofilo Cabastrero, a Spanish-speaking priest living and working in Nicaragua, "Blood of the Innocent" had been published in Britain by Catholic Institute for International Relations—a body which has a fine reputation internationally for fairness, independence and accuracy. (Orbis Books: US). I'd had it signed by some of the church leaders who had been part of the peacemaking ventures to Balmoral and Downing Street.

Why was the Cardinal so adamantly against the Sandinistas? Why did he appear to be supporting the contras? What would he make of the anguish in Cabastrero's book? What did he think of Archbishop Romero, the Salvadoran church leader who, despite his own conservative beginnings, had denounced the killings by the National Guard in El Salvador, and so had himself been killed, while saying mass? Why was he so against the 'popular church', that phenomenon of the present day churches which was bringing heaven down to earth, pitching into the struggle for water and land and food here and now, not buying people off with a possible future filled with celestial pie?

The Cardinal was not at home: not to me at any rate. The British Chargé d'Affaires, Robert Owen, proved very hospitable, plying me with tea (English Breakfast) from his own private stock. (It was almost worth going to see him for this alone: lukewarm coffee, black and sick-sweet, was standard in Nicaragua: tea was rare.) We spent several hours discussing the British position on Nicaragua. For him the whole US strategy was a mess, and Britain, but for her need to keep in with Reagan and the rest, should not have been associating with it. He seemed quite open about it all, even showing me part of a dispatch to Geoffrey Howe, the British Foreign Secretary, which said much the same thing. Predictably he did not think too much of the Sandinistas, but even so felt the US had blown the whole threat thing out of all proportion. The Nicaraguans should be left to find their own way. He did not approve of the peace march: diplomacy was the better way, but he respected our right to be in Central America, and what we were trying to do.

"Diplomacy sends honest men abroad—and turns them into liars. After all, one does have a mortgage to pay." This remark, half-humourous, echoed grimly through the Iran-Contra hearings: Robert MacFarlane, pressed as to why he hadn't opposed support for the contras he considered illegal, whimpered: "I was afraid Cap (Weinberger) and the others would think me some kind of commie." So is policy made. So the children of Central America go to the flames. And the tea cups clink.

The rest of the marchers were trying to get to El Salvador. Nicaragua and Salvador have no land border, so we had planned to go in through Honduras. With the slamming shut of the border at El Espino, our path to El Salvador was also blocked.

Attention focussed on the Gulf of Fonseca.

On the Pacific side of the continent, the gulf is little more than a large bay. Its shoreline is Salvadoran to the north, Honduran in the east, and Nicaraguan to the south. So, by taking ship at Potosi, in northwest Nicaragua, we could sail across the bay, miss Honduras altogether, and land on the beach in El Salvador.

Another group of delegates flew off for San Salvador, to link up with our supporters there, just as we had in Honduras. Just in time. The next day freedom-loving El Salvador also clamped its borders closed.

Once again we were back in the peace camp business. The expedition to Potosi was set up anyway: small dugout boats plied across the gulf, and, if we went up in our buses, rehired from the long-suffering Nicaraguan people, we could climb aboard and they could dump us over on the beach. These boats had a very bad safety record (as did the sharks in the gulf!), so I was glad to have my own little project going on to keep me in Managua (still tapping away at the Cardinal's door). Everyone else set off. They were back within the day.

The Salvadoran government let it be known that, if we launched ourselves out into the gulf, that would be an act of aggression by Nicaragua. The dugouts would be met with warships—the consequences were up to us! Once again we were persuaded to stop by the Nicaraguans, chasing after the buses.

It was not surprising that Honduras and El Salvador were so set against our coming. Quite apart from the horribly routine disappearances and killings so well documented in Salvador, there had been almost continuous US troop movements during the past three years in supposedly independent Honduras; and political repression was mounting. Then all the contra bases: a blind person would see too much.

Isn't it tragic that what is presented to us as the defence of democracy is in fact a war to destroy a courageous attempt at real popular participation: the people's labour, their own land, their own fruits? It was this lying, coupled with the suppression of the Costa Rica Libre affair and the tremendous freedom to question and to challenge in Nicaragua, which made us see just how deep the poison has run. The revelations of 25 years of 'Secret Team' wars, the foreign policy of the North's greed being conducted by the unelected little Norths, could be no surprise after all that.

But why? Are we really so afraid? Life for *all* the children. People free to choose their own friends, their own alliances. Homes and education. If we respond so violently to such dreams, isn't something deeply wrong? With us, with our system?

Other faint possibilities appeared. Someone was in touch with a banana boat going up the coast—but not for three more weeks. One of the Greenpeace ships was coming in close: we tried to contact it, but again nothing...

The energy was draining from the march. Money was becoming a problem: our original budgets had covered bus transport only. There were no boats, the road was blocked. We had to fly. But air tickets were expensive. Many decided to stay on in Nicaragua, travelling, working, joining the coffee and building brigades, seeing more people, asking more questions. Others went sadly home.

Others, determined to get to Guatemala and Mexico, scratched around to find the extra cash or had it wired out from home.

I went to see Robert Owen at the British Embassy.

Cardinal Obando y Bravo had agreed to a meeting at last. But not for two more weeks. By then I'd be long gone, up in Washington DC, trying to hand "Blood of the Innocent" over to Mr. Reagan.

Instead of the date with the Cardinal, I cadged $200 from Mr. Owen, and headed for the airline office.

We were invited to take part in one last intercultural event. These had been happening all over the place, deliberately planned sometimes, at others spontaneous. This one was special: it was our leaving party, and it was to be held in the cultural centre in downtown Managua. The heart of the city was razed in a massive earthquake in 1972. Somoza kept the disaster relief money. So 'downtown' is a vast empty space, a wasteland surrounding the triangular bulk of the earthquake proof Hotel Intercontinental: the local incarnation of the international gravy train.

The cultural centre had been the ground floor of
Somoza's favourite hotel. Open to the sky since the earthquake, but with the arches of the walls still standing,
painted gleaming white and brightly lit, it made a wonderfully dramatic setting. Singing Victor's songs there, for all
the people whose voices had been silenced, whose names
nobody knew, in that place where once only Somoza and his
rich friends had disported—that was really something.

The following evening I left—headed for Washington
via Mexico City.

Managua's airport is way outside the city. The flight for
Mexico left at 6 am, so I took a ride out with some other
marchistas who were leaving the evening before. Thanks to
past contra attacks the airport closed its doors at 9 pm. My
plan was to sleep outside on the grass until it opened up in
the morning. (It's another interesting commentary on the
real world—contrasted with that of the disinformers—that
it was quite safe to do this in Nicaragua: it is *not* safe in Los
Angeles or New York or London or even Edinburgh. In the
same way the women said they felt at ease, even on their
own and at night. Again in which of our free cities can they
claim that today?)

Having seen the others off, I was just getting ready to go
out into the dark, when a young woman came over to me.
She was one of a team of people who had been cleaning the
building: with a wide smile and merry eyes. She must have
been about 15, slight, dark, vibrant. My Spanish was still
appalling, and she spoke no English. But Valentina was her
name, and, once she'd discovered that I was a marchista, she
was determined that I should not sleep out on the ground.
Within moments I was the centre of a huddle: all her
friends from the cleaning, a couple of security men, airport
staff. It was decided: Valentina would take me home, and
bring me back in the morning. She said she lived really
close: 'muy cerca,' and, among peals of laughter about how
close we might get in the night, they hoisted me and my

gear into the truck which came by to drop everyone off. 'Muy cerca' turned out to mean the end of the line, right back in Managua.

By then I was too tired to care: there'd be another plane, another day. President Reagan could wait.

Valentina's little house I'd seen a thousand times before—in OXFAM posters. Tin roof, cardboard walls, one tap, one light bulb, one toilet out in the back yard. In one corner her mother and father were sleeping under their mosquito net, while from behind a makeshift partition Valentina produced a whole row of smaller brothers and sisters, who shyly shook my hands as she introduced us. Without any fuss she pulled down a bed spring from the wall, probably her own, put a mattress on it and a couple of blankets, smiled at me not to worry, and retired behind the screen.

Before dawn she reappeared with coffee and bread, together with her mother. Laughing they pulled me out of the house, lugging my rucksack behind them, clapping my hat on to my head. With a wave, her mother saw us on to the bus which came rumbling out of the darkness. Valentina paid the fares. We then took two taxis in succession: it was a long way. Again she paid, refusing all my attempts to offer money. We arrived at the airport in perfect time. I had plenty of dollars (thanks to the British Embassy!) but no cordobas, the Nicaraguan currency. Valentina could have got a good price for dollars on the black market, but refused over and over. Her purse was pitifully thin—her wages must have been tiny in that beleaguered economy. All she asked was that I take her picture. She gave me a big hug. Then, with a final grin, she disappeared to get herself home.

> Ay, Nicaragua, Nicaraguita
> La flor más linda de mi querer
> Abonada con la bendita

Nicaraguita
Sangre de Diriagen
Ay, Nicaragua, sos más dulcita
Que la mielita de Tamagas

Pero ahora que ya sos libre
Nicaraguita
Yo te quiero mucho más
Pero ahora que ya sos libre
Nicaraguita
Yo te quiero mucho más

Oh Nicaragua, Nicaraguita
Oh lovely flower, flower of my heart
Overflowing with purest waters
Nicaraguita
The blood of Diriangen
Oh Nicaragua, you're so much sweeter
Than all the honey of Tamagas

But now, my darling, my Nicaraguita
Now that you've freedom
My love for you can blaze out like fire
But now, my darling, my Nicaraguita
Now that you've freedom
My love for you can blaze out like fire!

(Nicaragua, Nicaraguita: Carlos Mejia Godoy)

While we were stalled up above Esteli, Carlos Godoy, Nicaragua's Victor Jara, came to sing for us. He was in Esteli to give concerts and to visit his family, for he had been born there. We all knew who he was, we'd seen him singing at the big public rallies around the country. He and his band of musicians came several times to play concerts under the stars, and gave us 'Nicaragua, Nicaraguita' to carry away with us home. I sing it at nearly all my own concerts still, and always it brings Valentina back to me, standing smiling in the morning sun outside the airport, making real in her own person all the generous independence of this little country, still laughing and singing in the face of all the odds. Embodying the music, she too cut through all the differences: wealth, language, culture, colour, gender: saying, with utter simplicity: "We are friends."

I had 3 days in Mexico city, waiting to pick up the Washington connection.

It was such a relief to find toilets that flushed, shops packed with food, cafes which boasted milk, and even tea! But what was happening to Roberto in Costa Rica, facing life with only one eye? Had Valentina been able to make up some of the wages she'd spent on the taxi fares? What of the dancing children in Esteli? And the superabundance, modest enough by British or US standards, was quickly repulsive, remembering the trade embargo and the empty shelves of the Nicaraguan shops, their economy devastated by the imposed war, the children going through our garbage to find extra food.

From Mexico the plane dropped me off, inconveniently, in Montreal, Canada (something to do with spare seats and cheap tickets). I was to join an international delegation from the march in Washington. (After overflying Honduras, the marchers formed up again in Guatemala, and completed the last leg into Mexico without too much difficulty. The final rally in Mexico City was huge—50,000.) I would have loved to have been in Guatemala and Mexico with everyone else, but "Blood of the Innocent" was burning a hole in my pocket, and I needed the ten days in Washington to organise getting to Mr. Reagan.

From Montreal I took a Greyhound bus down through New England, New York, Philadelphia and into Washington. The US officials at the Canadian border gave me a really rough time. I made the mistake of being honest: explaining that I was coming to talk with organisations and church people engaged in peace and justice work. I nearly laughed out loud when they started asking me whether I was a member of the Communist party, "Or have you ever been?"! They were in deadly earnest, especially on finding the Nicaraguan stamp in my passport. Luckily I had letters of accreditation from a variety of church and other leaders, and had sent the copy of "Blood of the Innocent" on to Washington by post. They read everything I was still carrying, including chunks of the journal I'd been keeping on the march. Somehow they missed all the anti-US remarks in it, but they threatened to phone Scotland anyway, to check my story out. As a climactic absurdity, they found a bottle of headache tablets in my medicine bag: "What have we got here?" one snarled: "Narcotics?"

It was like Keystone cops, except these guys could stop me dead in my tracks.

They did let me in, in the end, for a grudging two weeks (the normal visitor permit is for 6 months), and, with the bus growing rapidly more impatient outside, I stuffed everything back (they simply turned away without a word, leaving all my stuff strewn all over the counter) and walked gingerly out, expecting to be recalled at every step.

It's unlikely that anyone was checking out the march thousands of miles from the US/Mexican border, and I was more than a week early anyway. It was probably just the combination of the 'leftist' words peace and justice and that little passport stamp from Nicaragua which got them going. Whatever it was, it gave my tottering faith in the genuine depth of our democracy another serious jolt.

Pitching up in the centre of Washington, I had two

addresses. One was right around the corner. I went to look for it: the White House, ultimate source of so much of the anguish we'd seen. The second was only a phone number. Facing the White House I found a call box: "Hi, this is CISPES," said a voice. Minutes later I was sitting in the offices of the Committee In Solidarity with the People of El Salvador, and Barbara was fixing me coffee, a sandwich, a desk and a phone. Picking up where Valentina had left off, she took me home to stay with her and Jorge, her Salvadoran 'compa.'

The first thing was to try to get on the President's agenda.

It's another sad commentary on relations between our leaders and the people they claim to represent that, whenever I get to this point in the story, everyone falls about with laughter. And, of course, I'm forced to smile with them: "Get to see the President, leader of the world's greatest democracy? Don't be ridiculous!"

In one way the whole point of actions like the Marcha lies precisely in that ridiculousness. A challenge to what we accept too readily as the 'real world.'

I have a wonderful photo, taken at the Honduran border: it's from Nicaragua, into Honduras. Across the road the taut line of soldiers, standing guard, "Welcome to Honduras" signs behind them; in front, the marchers, sitting. Between, a juggler—juggling, disarmingly, for peace.

We asked the US consul in Managua: Why does the US go on supplying the contras, when the World Court of Justice has condemned their actions under international law; when so many US citizens are clearly saying that that support is unjust; and when all independent factfinding bodies condemn the US behaviour? Why?" His answer was: "It's a policy decision: in the real world we have to keep pressure on the Sandinistas."

What the juggler and the march were all about, what

Valentina said loud and clear, and why it was so important to get "Blood of the Innocent" to Mr. Reagan, was that policies end in people: irreplaceable, unique, yet profoundly connected. Presidents and others such spend their days taking policy advice and decisions; they think they have no time to meet the people those decisions affect. For the US the contra policy is, at best, a way to pressure the Sandinistas. For the people of Esteli it is the murderers coming over the hill to cut throats and skin alive; to rape and to machine gun.

Which is the *real* real world, for heaven's sake?

I caught snatches of a song the other day at an open air concert. The chorus, floating above the hubbub of the crowd, was:

> And the war is *real*
> and it's *really* intervention
> And the children *really die*
> as the bombs fall from the sky

It was to let the President hear the voices of those children that we had to try to reach him directly, and with the direct testimonies of that book.

"All the accounts of the men and women I listened to, most of them poor, went straight into my note pad or my tape recorder and from there to these pages. I treated the words of these people with the sacred respect due the blood, death, grief, terror, desperation, and tears of the poor.

"The speakers are innocent, defenseless victims of a truly 'dirty' war. This chronicle is an attempt to gather up their innocent blood, their murdered or violated or shattered lives, their unknown tragedy.

"Innocence and blood have names—first names and last names, and the names of events. But they can be summed up in a scream—a scream demanding that this war stop, that peace come to the land.

"I was struck by the great detail with which the campesinos, who always spoke to me with grief and sometimes with terror and tears, remembered all these events, all the things that they themselves, their families, their cooperatives, or their communities had suffered. They knew the importance of an exact account. They knew that this was history. A survivor of a massacre near Wiwili, a man whose whole being spoke of grief, told me: 'You see, I'm alive to tell the story so that the whole world will know.'

"And so I have decided to leave the accounts of my 'witnesses'—the suffering, the martyred—untouched, right down to the least details. I shall accord these accounts the respect due to legal documents or the Acts of the Martyrs. For this is what they are. They are the truthful records of the spilling of innocent blood.

"They constitute testimony that the grief and human pain of Nicaragua are more noble and worthy of respect, more daily, more concrete, and more complex—and the injustice of this war more cruel and human—than the world dreams.

"In Esteli I met Santos Roger. He had the face, voice and shyness of an adolescent. He told me 'I'm in school. I've finished my elementary education. I wanted to go and pick coffee to help the country's economy a bit. So I joined my brother's brigade. He was the chief. I wanted to go in a group.' He spoke slowly, with great concentration, and sometimes with such emotion that he would perspire and his voice would break off. Here is the story Santos told.

'There were 35 of us. It was a Tuesday. At 7:45 am we got into the truck to go and pick coffee in La Dalia, in San Juan, on the Coco River. Ten minutes later, as we passed through El Pericon, we were ambushed. A small

truck with some armed civilians was ahead of us, to
protect us while we were picking, and they let that truck
through. They opened fire on our truck, though, with
machine guns, LAU RPG-7 rocket launchers, and rifles.
The truck kept going about another 300 meters until a
rocket blew out its tires and it went down a ravine. It
was still right-side-up, but some of our people were
already dead. I got out of the truck somehow and
dragged myself along for a few meters. Then I played
dead. The contras came up to the truck and cut
anybody's throat that was screaming. Then they set fire
to the truck, with some people still alive in it, including
a mother and her little kid, five years old, that we were
giving a ride to.

'Just a couple of meters from where I was lying was
one of the guys with both his legs shot up; he was
moaning. As they went by him they slit his throat with
a bayonet and then they machine-gunned him. I saw
them slit some wounded people's throats if they'd
jumped out of the truck, and then they machine-gunned
them.

'And then I heard the screams of the wounded ones
inside as they were burning alive.'

'My name is Audilia Hererra de Ochoa. I'm a widow.
I'm 53. I'm a practising Christian. I lived in a village
called Los Terreros, 18 kilometers from Yali. We had to
have eyes in the back of our head. We could never work
or sleep peacefully. One day the contras came, rousted
us out, and said: 'Come out of there. You're all going to
be shot. Get into the fields, because these houses are
going to burn . . .' Right on the spot, as they were going
from house to house, they grabbed a poor guy who had
army boots on—but he was retarded, I mean severely
retarded—and they killed him right on the spot. They
cut his throat. That was the first terrible thing I saw . . .

The terror, the horror, when those people have come through your village . . . Without so much as a by-your-leave, the leader goes into the other room and starts going through papers. My girls held school there—it was an adult education center. They burned our papers, books notebooks, everything they could lay their hands on . . .

'Then they wanted to take my husband with them. But I told them: 'If you take him take me too. If he's going to pay for something he didn't do, we'll both pay. We're two in one flesh . . .' But I couldn't make it. I was too sick. They took my husband and left the rest of us there.

'The next day my husband came home. 'Work,' they'd said. 'Don't meddle.' Then I said, fine, we've been cleared. We can breathe easy.

'But one night someone came knocking at the door. It was them. They had a list of names. They already had everybody else they wanted in the valley and now they wanted me and my daughter. I wouldn't budge. We fought, and they took my daughter. They raped her. Apparently the whole troup wanted to get her and then they'd kill her, because that's what they did to a cousin of mine, fourteen years old; a lot of guys raped her and then they killed her. But they didn't have time to finish when they had my daughter. The army came up on them and they had to fight. Then when the mortars started, a chief, it was Zacarias, gave the order: 'Every man for himself!' And my daughter got away . . .'

'There's a co-op in the valley. There was a horrible massacre there. They killed eleven year old kids. I saw the atrocities. They murdered people and committed all sorts of abominations. And then they wear medals and crosses and carry a Bible! And they say they pray before committing their evils and Jesus tells them they're

going to win! 'That's Satan talking to you,' I told them.
'Your war hasn't got a future. Go to work, you men,
don't be so lazy.'

'So when I see that those people have Reagan's
support and financing, I don't know what Señor Reagan
is after. It must be to finish us all off, people who don't
do anything to him, people who eat their bread with
sweat on their faces, little people, people with no
power, people only looking for beans and corn so they
can live in peace, people trying to make something of
themselves. I don't see how that man can be so lacking
in conscience and not stop to think that there's a God
who wants us to live too. He's never stopped to consider
that . . . Doesn't he think he's ever going to die? Mr.
Reagan has left so many widows and orphans in this
land. Lord, does he believe in God and not see that?'"

(Blood of the Innocent: Padre Teofilo Cabastrero)

I dropped an urgent letter into the White House mail
room, carefully enclosing the names of all the signatories.
The person who received it said she would walk it across to
the President's office herself. Then, through CISPES, we
enlisted Congressman Ron Dellums to help with expediting
things.

Of course we were not *so* unrealistic as to expect that the
President would be able to see anyone, bishops and Dellums
notwithstanding, within the couple of weeks I had been
granted. All we were after, in the first instance, was some
indication of willingness to at least accept the book. (Could
we have held out against one of the officials in the Latin
American office, for example, accepting it for the
President?)

We go no reply.

I delivered another letter, this time expressing willing-

ness to come back at any time in the future, even six months
hence.

Nothing.

(An 'answer' did eventually come to this: long after I'd
returned to Scotland. It came via the US Consul in London.
It ran:

"The President wishes me to thank you for expressing
your opinion"!)

Reading glumly through the news one day, I saw Jesse
Jackson was to be in town. Now, could it be...? He had
been very supportive of the march...

Suddenly it was Balmoral all over again, letters and
phone calls and all night sessions. Except this time a
completely different world: the obstacles were no longer
ancient tradition and the refined art of inaction, but the
manic bustle and ironclad schedules of superheated politics.

Another long story. Anyway, we did it. Jackson would be
on Capitol Hill for a news conference: 2 pm, January 26th
(1986). He had a plane out at 4:30. Could we hand "Blood of
the Innocent" over at 3:00 pm?

Could we!!?

Dellums' staff got us a room in the same Congress
building that Jackson was using for his own conference. I
spent a feverish week writing and distributing press
releases: detailing the character of the book, and the
weightiness of the signatories; telling how the White
House wasn't even replying; telling about the march. We
hit the jackpot: ABC and CBS News teams said they'd cover
the handover, and we even got the McNeil/Lehrer
Newshour, the US's most prestigious mainstream current
affairs programme, on the line.

Came the day: the phones were humming, everything
set. I went out to pick up some lunch around 12 and rode the
tiny elevator back to the CISPES floor. The lift attendant

had his radio bleating on. "Any news?" "Nope. Nothing much. Except some little plane crash down south somewhere: Florida maybe." "Anyone hurt?" "Well, maybe six or seven killed, I guess."

As plane crashes go...But...wait a minute! As I stepped our of the lift I *knew* it: that 'little plane' had to be the Challenger space shuttle, timed to lift off that very morning. And, besides the regular crew, it was carrying Christa MacAuliffe, the young all-American teacher who had starred for weeks on chatshows, who was going to give her children the first ever lesson from space.

Back in the office, the worst fears...lifting off on its gargantuan wave of hype, the shuttle had torn itself to pieces after just 70 seconds, live on TV sets right across the nation.

The phones died: no one was calling anymore. How could the murder of countless 'Latinos' just trying to make a life for their families hope to compare in newsworthiness with a young pretty teacher going where few 'men had gone before,' and dying in the venture?

This was the real world after all.

We kept our tryst with Jesse Jackson. Amazingly, for a moment, the way to our room was knee deep in cameras and technicians and anchorpeople. They weren't looking for us: they were waiting for the Science and Technology Committee, meeting in emergency session.

I still feel like weeping as I write. Of course what happened to Christa MacAuliffe and her companions was terrible. Even though they were playing their parts in a massive promotion for the space programme, failing in public interest and packed with militarism, their deaths were terrible, tragic.

But did every reporter in Washington have to drop everything else to pile into the scrum to pick over the pieces? Did nothing else matter in the whole world? Didn't any newsperson care, couldn't any single one of them see, that this was perhaps the one chance these unnamed ones were going to get to have their stories told across the nation? That, for just this once, maybe the real real world could break through the fantasies of 'Star Trek' and the President's 'Star Wars,' and ordinary US people could hear what their government was doing, in their name, to other ordinary people—who just happened to be Nicaraguans.

And the subtext: every bit as tragic were the vast resources bayed up at the moon, while, on earth, half the people went hungry.

We waited forlornly in the empty room: no MacNeil or Lehrer, no ABC, no CBS. 3 pm came and went: no Jesse Jackson. 3:30. We collected our papers up; the copies of "Blood of the Innocent" we'd scoured the Washington stores to have ready for release to the press: all those voices waiting to be heard.

At 3:40 a woman appeared in the doorway: "Is this where the Reverend Jackson was supposed to be at 3 o'clock?" she asked breathlessly. "Well, he's just outside, and about to miss his plane. Would you come and meet him on his way to the front door?"

We ended up cooped together in the elevator, him apologising for the delay (the shuttle had virtually wiped out his own press conference too: they scraped a few seconds in after the statement from the Technology committee), and me stumblingly asking him to accept the book on behalf of the signatories, above all for the people of Nicaragua. And could he pursue it with the administration? The doors flung open in a welter of bodyguards, a quick stop in the foyer for a hurried photo (Barbara had fixed this too), and, thrusting the book into an aide's hands, Jackson was gone.

Nothing can retrieve that disaster.

But three things remain.

Barbara, Jorge and the others who befriended me.

The fact that, thanks to the White House's intransigence, I am now living here, at a new level of intensity and involvement.

And singing 'Prayer to the Labourer' at the Vietnam memorial wall. Washington had killed Victor by backing the murderers in Chile. His songs, with their luminous beauty and unquenchable spirit, had brought thousands into the struggle, and even to the gates of the White House itself.

"Stand up and see...reach out...by deepest blood united." The words broke over the wall, became people pressing against the gates: Victor himself, Valentina, Roberto, Sheila, Frank...all the unnamed ones—Cutumay's cloud of 'unconquerable sparrows'..."knowing together the future can be now!"

Journal at the Frontline 7

November 15th

We've had a lot of activity, protesting the murder of Sanabria. No more killing so far, although the threats continue. Again, what have his children and his wife done? What did he do, for heaven's sake???

(Again it makes me angry: "You couldn't hold these protests in the Soviet Union." How often do you hear that? But who's listening? Protests can be a very effective way to control letting off steam. Freedom of speech is a two-way thing. To be real there has to be a genuinely open ear: people must listen—and that is hardly the most obvious attribute of our present babble of politicians.)

A great honour: I've been asked to play and sing at a reception for Cutumay Camones in a few days time.

November 19th

Yesterday the evening with Cutumay. I was about the only gringo there. Hall jam-packed. It was a very Salvadoran affair: a family party. I sang Victor, of course, and "Nicaragua, Nicaraguita." (I didn't dare one of Cutumay's own songs, and Salvadorans cheer for Nicaragua almost as loudly as they do for El Salvador.)

The whole group was there, although they didn't perform together: a family reception for favourite brothers and sons—and one sister/daughter. Cutumay is one of the few groups which has a woman in the line-up.

Good for women's rights, for all our balance, good for the musical texture—much the richer for her voice.

The principal singer, Eduardo (who it turns out, comes originally from Holland—so I am on the right lines: he's married to a Salvadoran lass. I should be so lucky!), took a guitar and sang some of their most popular songs, just himself, sweetly and simply. He was so good!

He writes most of the songs too: what a musician! Since living with the family I've been able to appreciate how fine they are. And he has a lovely voice.

That I should ever have been asked to sing!

Talking of 'all our balance,' it makes me laugh. Yanira is zooming round like a mad thing. Far from the threats stopping her work, she's stepped it up: she's become the co-ordinator of UMSL—right out front.

So here's me, the longtime male executive, staying home typing her letters and minding the children, while Yanira dances with death, speaking, travelling, organising, confronting . . .

This switcharound, plus the stretching of our family from Scotland to El Salvador via Nicaragua, Chile, England, the US, is the 'revolution' happening: one world, one people, one family. Friendship, enduring love between equal partners. Women and men together, co-responsive with, and responsible to, one another no matter where we're born, sharing life as naturally as a parent shares food with her children, holding the whole fragile earth in our arms.

It's lovely: I'm starting to feel at home, everywhere. Here I've been given special names: 'Apolonio,' 'Paulito.' Carlito calls me 'Peep'.

December 1st

*So far no word from the immigration department. My
permit ran out on October 23rd! I got my renewal
application in really late—after the deadline. I'm kind of
scared of forms anyway, and put it off. Plus we're sure the
CIA/FBI have tabs on us. How much of what I'm doing
will transfer between computers, I wonder? But, after the
public relations disaster for US/Salvador support, which
the death squad attacks here have turned into, I don't
think they'll bother to cancel me. It just wouldn't be worth
their while—anything to do with Yanira is probably
hands-off for now. (Already the effects of good old
Scottish/British muscle was shown when folk wrote from
home to LA Mayor Bradley, asking why we weren't
getting any noticeable police protection. Within a few
days, the local station was on the line . . . the support from
home has been great.)*

*I hope that's right! I'd be sick if I got sent home on a
technicality for going over time. I shouldn't have given
that opening. Stupid.*

*One thing: everyone says the department takes so long
to process any application, I'll probably make another 6
months' stay before they even get back to me.*

December 8th

*Twenty-five years ago today Nunraw signed me on.
Little did the monks know how much they were giving
me: from silence and solitude to chaos and war; from the
rolling hills, silent under the snow to the desecrated
desert, locked in concrete, asphyxiating in smog. Heaven
to earth. Timid isolationist to wandering minstrel. Music*

all the way.

Where will the next 25 go? I'm feeling more and more at home here, with the whole family and community of Salvadorans in struggle. And so many things seem to have come to an end in Scotland: Barbara gone; Shindig needing to move on; SEAD out of money for me—and anyway our perspectives increasingly divergent: the committee for increased 'professionalism': specialisation, rank, salary; me for seemingly more radical ways: equals within a co-operative structure, money divided 'to each according to need' (what we do with our money always seems to be such a touchstone).

There's Mother and Father and the rest of the family of course, but I've been stuck away up in Scotland for years, with everyone else down around Bath, in Southwest England. It takes about as long to get from here to Bath, door to door, as from Edinburgh. Crazy!

Maybe as well all my fulminating against colonialism is being challenged. Perhaps what we need now is colonialism in reverse, people going out from the North, to relearn the true civilisation of making again "every tree an object of reverence". I can fix houses after all; and learn songs; help organise; write articles. What makes growing sense is for me to stay with Leticia and Co., coming and going regularly from Britain (6 months here in the US, 2 months there?), serving as a living channel in both directions. To transfer information, encouragement, music, support . . .And when 'el triunfo' comes, to go back to Salvador with them to help rebuild the lives shattered by the war—this war driven by the demands (coffee, bananas, hamburgers, arms) of our tawdry golden calves: More and More.

And to carry on the musical yo-yoing.
Of course. It'll be the more important then. Salvador
will have to build a humane society from scratch.
Endurance. We mustn't do the usual thing of turning away
to new trendier causes, once the day of revolution has
come and gone. As the Central Americans all say: the
revolution is a process, throwing out the dictators is just
the beginning.

Funny to think everyone's getting ready for Christmas
over there in Britain (talking of "More and More!");
better get a few cards written.

Christmas Day

Didn't get that many cards off . . . But spoke with Mum
and Dad, and quite a few other pals—international calls
are amazingly cheap: only about 60 cents (35p?) a minute.
Global village or what?

Mother and Father seem well enough. It's sad not to be
with them. Father's 81 now and Mother will be 80 next
birthday. How is that possible? I must try to be in Bath for
her birthday. They've seemed set to go on forever. But
suddenly they say they're feeling much older. Trust me to
take off for the other side of the world. At least the rest of
the family is close. Being apart is part of war too.
What can it be like for Leticia, having seen what they
did to Yanira and still with family in El Salvador?

January

The new year has brought a little more space. Not quite
so much pressure on us. Reading this journal over, it's

difficult to take in the intensity of the past months, and to realise there's a great big country out there busily getting on with life, squads or no squads.

It was in Washington that I first realised how there is a rightwing party here (Democrats) and an extremely rightwing party (Republicans). And that's compared with Britain—where one can hardly describe the present pale Labour Party as radically socialist!

(Isn't that strange: why is this country so reactionary? After all the modern US was born in revolution, so short a time ago. The white settlers did terrible things to the indigenous peoples and their culture—but they must have had some courage and fire to come all those thousands of miles in their miserable little boats: and to a completely unknown land.

But then: wasn't it leave or die for so many? And weren't they countryfolk and small craftspeople—traditionally conservative? Also many were driven to flight to preserve their fundamentalist Christianity: looking for somewhere to worship their various versions of god in peace.

Poor 'Indians': whose peace? Even Woody Guthrie's "This Land is Your Land"—that 'anthem of the people'—ignores them and their fate. What happened to them is the touchstone.

Maybe it's not so surprising that the US is so conservative. I wonder. What do I really know about it?)

Anyway the most recent political joke was the 'race' for president (a case for a Steward's Enquiry if ever . . .). An article in the Los Angeles Times (faintly left of the rightwing center) ran the title: "If You Hope To Be President, Big, Bold, Interesting Ideas Just Get You Into Trouble" (who needs the article?). George Bush, vice-

president to the "Great Lia . . ." oops, pardon me!*. . . Great* Communicator" *(for blank read Reagan), was the hot tip to follow in the great man's fatuities. He ran a foully mean campaign, Dukakis was wiped out, and Bush is now calling for a "kinder, gentler nation." He's not noted for ideas at all, let alone big ones. He sold himself on his loyalty to Reagan (wrong thing for the wrong reason, to turn Elliott in his grave). Jesse Jackson, who has put on some (political) weight since our fleeting encounter in the Washington elevator, was deemed "unelectable" (the Media's way of telling us not to vote for him?) He's black of course here in the great home of freedom and democracy, plus he also seems to have ideas. Bad.*

If politics were just about illusion and froth, it wouldn't matter: we could all afford presidents who'd be good party turns as illusionists. But, of course, while Mr. Reagan was acting (?) the buffoon (he recently appeared as straight-man to Bob Hope. Is that possible? Or am I the only person in the world who finds Mr. Hope himself grindingly unamusing?), his policies were exterminating people, destroying economies and overturning elected governments. Mr. Reagan and Mr. Hope made the headlines on nationwide TV: what was happening during their act, through their mediums of the contras and the death squads, did not. Needless to say.

How different can Bush be? Will he be allowed to be? If he is the nice guy that a lot of people claim, and genuinely out to make the US kinder, how to account for the virulence of the campaign? The Directorship of the CIA? The years of loyalty to Reagan? Where was George during Iran/Contra? His "Read my lips" has become TV folklore. No tax hikes, of course. But, way before that, those same lips, thin and whipping with malice, made me shiver as he derided those he had labelled liberals.

We'll see. At least Reagan took his ideological soulmate (Abrams not Nancy) with him when he went. Maybe with those two gone (to say nothing of the lady's astrologers!) some sort of sense may be allowed to butt into the Central American scene. Any bets?!
By their fruits . . .

It's sickening. Yanira has started trying to get work as a house cleaner. She's forced to do this in spite of her still unhealed wounds, and on top of all her constant work for her people—to pay the huge medical bills: for what the thugs did to her. The Reagan/Hope duo were farting about at some plush funding do: thousands, maybe millions of dollars. We managed to scrape $1,500 for the replacement car, and are struggling along at a hundred or so a week. They wouldn't bother to pick that up.

And all for what they did to her.

The major operation looks more and more likely: she's still only 23.
$15,000-$20,000.

Yani says she has Carlito, and that she'll adopt war orphans when we go back to El Salvador.
I bet she will too.

7 My Own Revenge...
Mi Venganza Personal

"Como gorriones invincibles . . . "

Farm and factory workers
Women and students
—All of us together
Like unconquerable sparrows

"While they were hurting me there came a moment
when all I could think was: 'Kill me: oh why don't you kill
me?'"

Yesterday, for the first time really since I've been here, I
heard Yani speak publicly about the attacks. We were at a
local church. It was unbearably moving: because of her
sweet directness; because they did these unspeakable things
to my own sister. And because, in the end, she refused to die.

"But the faces and names and voices of friends and
people I'd known who had been tortured and killed came
before my mind, and they had been so full of life, and now
they were dead. I was only 22; I could not let their memory
die, their work go for nothing; I had to go on living. They,
those dear dead ones, gave me back my life."

"You ask us why we sing": Yanira, Victor, Violeta, Pablo,
Gabriel, Sonia, Joanna, Ernesto, Carlito, Valentina. Mother
and Father holding us close under the bombs. Fillan lifting
me onto the tractor. Mark in the early dawn, helping work
the back of the guitar. Shindig. The eternal ache of the

chant and the flamenco. The countless nameless ones whose laughter and whose courage still echo in the silences which shimmer in the songs, still sound deep in the Soleares, "unending as the water weeps."

They leave us the music of their courage.

And their music, too, gives us back our life. It brings all the 'gorriones'—the little ones, the 'sparrows'—of the world together, welding us into one unity of heart and purpose, the destroyed ones with the living. And, in the singing, we know that we *are* invincible, that: 'our song and our silence *are* stronger than death, and that in the end, indeed they will *not* falter.'

This is our song in high summer, *this* is why we sing.

When Yanira finished speaking, she asked me for her favourite song again: Tomas Borgé's "Mi Venganza Personal: My Own Revenge." It says everything, she said.

"I will be revenged upon your children
When they've the right to schooling and to flowers
My vengeance will be sweet when I can sing you
This song born in the freedom and the quiet hours..."

and...

"When that day comes I'll greet you with 'Good Morning'
And there will be no beggars left to haunt us..."

and...

"For when you the one who tortured me stand forward
Your eyes downcast and all your strength forgotten
My revenge will be to reach to you my brother
With these the very hands which once you tore and tortured
Without the strength or power to rob them
of their tenderness"

To watch little Carlos sometimes, to see the loneliness and hurt and anguish bequeathed him by the thugs as he sat helpless in the car. And then to see his mother standing there speaking so lovingly, so serenely somehow. And to know that, for daring to dream her dream, for loving even those who tortured her, trying to bring schooling and freedom to their children as well as to her own son, she's again in the front line, again in so much danger. This is to know the war is real indeed.

It's a war of course to end the mayhem throughout the world caused by the decisions we allow certain minority representatives to take on our behalf in the comfortable seclusion of the Oval Office and Downing Street. Decisions worked out in proxy maiming and murder in the mountains of Esteli and on the streets of San Salvador and Los Angeles.

But, as 'Mi Venganza' shows, it's also a war for the spirit of all of us, for the heart of our civilisation. In fighting for themselves, Yanira and her compas are fighting for us too. The end to the war can only come when, contrary to so much that we have imbibed of 'charity' and even 'justice,' we climb off our self-constructed pedestal, and accept support and help from those we patronisingly brand 'underdeveloped.'

Shrivelled charity was never enough. How can we have thought it ever could be? Such charity presupposes and perpetuates difference: They are the 'Have-nots,' we are the 'Haves.' It's not our fault: for are not 'the poor always with us?' Our relative wealth comes to us abstractly, through our own efforts visited on a neutral world. Everyone has the same choices. Everyone has bootstraps, let them pull themselves up. *We* had to, didn't we? Since that wealth is ours, we can use it as we like. Good people are 'charitable' of course. Charity has always been the dismal ghost at the feast, reminding us of those 'less fortunate than ourselves' (Doesn't that give us away? We know perfectly well that there are millions of people who, work as they will, will barely manage sandals—let alone boots. Charity peers out at us from the posters of the starving children, charity jangles at us on the street corners in the rattling cans. Charity is really our response to the echo of guilt which chimes, now loud, now soft, but with spasmodic constancy, somewhere in the silence.

A oneway transaction, entered into (and withdrawn from) solely at the discretion of the donor, charity, this withered ghost of love, demands only that the recipient be needy and 'deserving.' S/he has no real role to play, other than to accept, and show proper gratitude. Charity is not allowed to make claims on the giver, its 'object' may be seen but should certainly not be heard. It is always easiest to practise when that object lives on the other side of the world.

Justice has begun to challenge charity's stranglehold on our response to the intrusions of the real world. Bella-houston, Balmoral and the journey through Central America are part of the development of a movement, which started with the simple determination to challenge the unending arming of the world, but which has begun to understand true peace is impossible without social justice. So it focuses increasingly on the redistribution of resources. Material resources, yes, of course, but also of shining intellect and whole working, creative lives, which, in our developed nations, are presently aborted into the lunacies of overwhelming weaponry and blinded consumerism. The 'development' agencies too have been moving away from the starving baby focus, challenging charity to look more closely at the distant sources of its apparent largesse, to see where the raw materials of our surpluses come from, and how those who grub them up are forced to live. To taste whose blood is on our money.

Justice is much better than charity.

Injustice is a 24 hour a day, 7 day a week way of death. Justice has to be as constant a force for life, we cannot pick and choose, changing with the wind. Justice knows that none of us lives in a neutral world, that so much of our own development has been—and continues to be—at the expense of other people, that whole peoples go to the wall to feed our growth. So, where charity speaks of 'the poor,' justice sees 'the dispossessed,' those who *are being* disinherited, right now, 24 hours a day, 7 days a week. And that they 'will be with us always' only if we so choose.

Justice is better—but it's still not enough. Justice is still too easy to 'do to' someone. There is a great gulf fixed: we will be just to you. Justice is still, often, immensely patronising.

Isn't it all *people* at the last? Justice only makes sense as part of the interchange of respect between equals: people, not mere statistics. It struck me so strongly—back from Central America—the great 'issues' had become particular flesh and blood, unique human beings, each with a name and a story. Somehow all the years of agonising and struggling, above all the songs and music, had borne final fruit.

The faces and the names had become my friends, giving me the courage to listen and to receive. Friendship *is* two-way: born of respect and equality. So, when we got home from Nicaragua, despite all the sad, terrible things we had seen, all the troubles we had endured, I found I was deeply rested.

Valentina, with her wonderfully warm generosity, exactly summed up the turning everything upside down. We armchair revolutionaries could relax: the popular movements in Nicaragua and El Salvador are threats indeed, but only to our patronising selfishness, only to our guilt and pride, only to our system which *can* live with beggars haunting us—not only from our TV screens and posters of the starving but in the doorways of our supermarkets, on the very pavement outside the White House. Once we realise that the Central Americans *will* be free— *are* already free, in so many ways—because of their own spirit and not because we decide to give them their freedom back—and that that is not a threat but an opportunity to flesh out our sketched-in democracy—to intensify it and make it more profound—then we can begin to relax.

But, of course, this relaxing is not about slumping down in front of the television with a can of beer (although part of it may well be knowing when, and how, to rest properly in order to stay the course to the very end). It's the relaxation of the athlete, of the singer, tuned and poised. It's the ease of the living silence between people who are deeply in love, who, at the heart of their lovely passion, have found gentleness and respect and utter trust. Far from being the escape from involvement and action which we have sold ourselves through the 'leisure business,' it is the timing and delicacy and poise of utter commitment, the glorious, all-consuming passionateness of every fresh "I love you."

By their befriending us, Victor, Valentina, Yanira and the rest are helping us to see how much of the White Man's Burden we still carry, and to begin to jettison it. Governors of much of the world in the heyday of Empire, we white peoples tried to justify our stealing and despoiling other peoples' lands by inventing this 'burden'—the self-imposed task of bringing our version of civilisation (primarily male and material) to poor, 'backward,' 'coloured,' Africa and Asia and Latin America. This patronising self-righteousness ripped the throat out of countless traditional cultures, together with their strongest children, sold into slavery directly or via indenture, and their most precious material resources, sucked into the relentless maw of northern industrialisation.

It claimed that the 'savages' were not fully human. The 'Dark Continents' were inhabited by 'Niggers,' 'Gooks,' 'Wops,' 'Indians.' (Isn't our Third World still? Here in California anyone from south of the border is 'mexican,' whether she be from Tijuana or Tierra del Fuego.) The world was full of coloured races (i.e.: every *other* colour but pasty pink/white). And, of course again, because 'they' were 'different' (inferior)—because God had so ordained things—they could be used as we whites saw fit (For tax — evasion—purposes, black people in the romantic South of "Gone With the Wind" were calculated to be exactly three fifths human).

All this is ingrained. Back in the Charterhouse I remember my own racist bile bursting. The monk who kept charge of the church was from India. He would look you up and down, with seeming coldness (probably his way to hold onto silence in his enforcedly public role). The first time I caught his glance such a virulence shot through me: "You black...why are you looking at me like that!!?" This not only there, 'in God's house,' but after I'd been living the blues and jazz of Johnny Dodds and Joe Oliver and Bessie Smith for years.

In our own time that burden has become the determination to 'develop' the 'poor'—no matter what.

This *is* often deeply commingled with genuine outrage, as when we young monks paced the newly minted cloisters, calculating how many homeless families we could shelter within their walls.

But how really does it meet our *joint* needs for justice? *Our* need to receive and to learn? To face up to reality?

What real chance was there that we would ever actually offer our cloisters for people's homes? And if we did, what point would there be for homeless city dwellers to be so marooned far into the wilderness?

Weren't the real questions: "How is it that we few monks, vowed to poverty, have more than a thousand acres and two huge houses at our disposal, while other people, our 'brothers and sisters in God,' have only the streets? What can the homeless ones tell us about our society— about ourselves? And how do we change things so that we *all* have enough?"

Aren't these still the real questions for us all? Why *do* we go on drinking and eating and laying the world waste as if our excesses and low prices had nothing to do with the unravelling of our environment and whole families withering under starvation wages and disease and malnutrition? Why do we go on accepting the lies and abrogation of basic freedoms—our own too—by which the crudely powerful maintain this massive injustice. Why are we so apathetic? So frightened? So ready to run to the advertisers and the pulp media to keep us safe from reality? So ready to accept the claptrap and the wholesale law-breaking with which so many politicians assure us they are 'defending democracy' and 'fighting for freedom'? To stop up our ears when Victor or Yanira try to tell us how their peoples are paying the price for all this 'freedom': what Noam Chomsky calls the unwritten "5th Freedom" of the US Constitution, that of plundering and destabilising any part of the world we claim is 'vital to our national interests and security'?

But, what are we to do? Where else do we start but with where we are, and with what we have?

When I came to Washington DC last, to stay for just the three weeks, I left the rubbish tip guitar in Scotland. It turned out to be more than a year before I got back to it, and because it hadn't been played in all that time, it had lost most of its lovely tone. I have it back with me now. Nursing it along, hearing its beauty gradually reawaken, I've relived something of the wonder of its original birth, cobbled together all those years ago from the monastic scraps and the surreptitious scrapings of the early morning.

But it also reminds me where the impulse to begin the making came from: that refusal to spend $100 to buy a guitar—because using it to sing about families who try to live on $100 a year would not ring true.

Coming from a culture so dominated by money, my seeing the problem in material terms was to be expected. To begin at all we *do* have to begin where we are. And money has its place.

But would I be here today if I'd just inveigled my family into buying an instrument?

Probably not.

Not so much because that original insight was right after all—I'm still not sure about it. It's more because of what the guitar itself taught me, incidentally almost, in the making. The creative offspinning of compassion.

It gave me back my hands, reconnecting them with my heart and my head in developing the carpentry skills which now help make a living within my adopted family—and one day will work in building people's houses in new El Salvador. It reawakened the imagination to find the beauty hidden under the dirt of the scraps. It gave me the feel and scent of wood, and the elegance of properly balanced tools.

The fact that we, poor monks again, could dump mahogany and oak, gave rise to an astonished anger at the throwing away of our entire planet in which we have all been so casually engaged.

The guitar gave me Mark's friendship, as we felled the diseased chestnut tree together and saved the slender slice to make the back.

This enduring beauty, emerging from such unlikely sources, has given birth to an abiding distrust of the creeping consumerism and 'expertisation' of society, which denies us so much of our own creativity by packaging things away from us: building a guitar or keeping fit or having a child. Politics too.

And now I have been given songs and friendship, a community, a world family: a whole way of life worth dying for. Who could ever claim that for consumerism?

The loveliness blossoming from that first stumbling step seems to go on forever. And this is part of what it's about, isn't it? Start where we are, certainly: take a first step, however small (even the greatest dancer stumbled over her first steps); then *keep* listening, *keep* expecting, *keep* going.

The guitar, small and personal as it is, is just one example of what we can all do if we decide to take back responsibility for our own lives. It says so much about our capacity for constructive change, for finding new life. For *life* finding *us,* given the chance.

Maybe it doesn't matter how partial the vision that gets us started, provided only that we *do* start. And *keep going.*

Each of us has to take that step for herself or himself—all the words in the world cannot do it for us. For all the excitement and fun and life that have been given to me, they remain profoundly personal, a song which only I can sing. But harmony is different songs sung to the same deep pulsing. Each of us has to find her own song, yes—the lovely paradox is that each individual song only sounds right within that overall harmony.

Recently I was in Boston and New England with Yanira on a speaking and singing tour. One of the songs we used was "What Have We Done To The Rain." Flying back over the Rockies, over the Grand Canyon, and over all the other marvels—the millions of people and all their lives—we were more or less forced into pulling down the window shades, to 'consume' a movie. It makes me feel as though we're all locked into a closed room: quite a pleasant room even, but airless and stifling with the shutters tightly sealed. Each one of us has a key to the door, but we rarely use it—through custom, through complacency, through fear.

Music and stories brought in from outside: about the warmth of the sun, singing the scent of the wind, bringing the flowers back home, petal by shining petal, drumming the raindrops into the surface of the sea, catching the echoes of the sufferings and laughter of the distant ones, all these can only be the beginnings of the great dream.

However powerful they may be, how can they compare
with that first reaching out, the unlocking of the door, the
actual *taking* of that first small step across the threshold,
feeling for the first time the warmth of the sun, *tasting* the
weeping of the rain, *being enfolded* in the scent of a rose?:

"Stand up and see the wonder of the mountain"

But how to break out? That first step, apparently so hard,
seemingly so hopeless—how to take it? We treat it as
though it were as absurd and dangerous as opening the door
of the plane and trying to walk along the wing.

Most of us have been moved by the pictures flickering in
the corner of the room. Most of us have responded to the
images of the starving and homeless. To the *images*. And so
we've sent off our cheques, maybe even joined with some
others in marching round the room carrying placards and
banners and calling on 'them' to do something.

That's a beginning.
But what then? And who are 'They?'
What really counts is have we moved any closer to the
door?

For all our marching have we allowed the real thing—
not the crap cola of the advertisements gluing our news
broadcasts together, but the flesh and blood people behind
the images—to come in, even for a moment? Often the
reverse. How often, after the marches, do we check
anxiously to see if we made it onto television (although we
decry the shallowness of the medium)? As if 'As Seen On
TV!' will give us ourselves too, just as it authenticates soap
powder and presidents: And we settle down again into our
comfortable chairs, our backs set firmly against the door.

I'm tucked into a corner of the living room writing this,
plucking the words out of the maelstrom of the children
getting their breakfast. Leticia is presiding over Susanna

and Carlos, serving them pancakes and honey. The little ones are great pals, although Carlito is forever getting Susanna into scrapes. He's nearly twice her age, and tries to dominate her, already showing signs of the machismo which Yanira laments so in Salvadoran society. He's currently trying to smear honey all over the table while Leti's back is turned: Susanita thinks it all hugely amusing, of course...

Hey! He's not just trying, he's... *Carlito!!!!!*

Because what's happened has made me a member of his family, adopted but real, he's stopped. (He's now surreptitiously feeding the dog!)

Surely the key is exactly that—that simple, natural, and hard all at once—one *family*.

Are we?

Or not?

For centuries religion has taught us that we are. But we never *really* believed it.

Did we?

If so, how to account for all the dark side of our civilisation: the slavery, of life or of wages, the 'economic necessity' for unemployment, for war, for debt, for global oppression?:

"...We have about 50% of the world's wealth, but only 6.3% of its populations...In this situation, we cannot fail to be the object of envy and resentment. Our real task in the coming period is to devise a pattern of relationships which will permit us to maintain this position of disparity without positive detriment to our national security. To do so we will have to dispense with all sentimentality and daydreaming; and our attention will have to be concentrated everywhere on our immediate national objectives. We need not deceive ourselves that we can afford today the luxury of altruism and world benefaction... *We should cease to talk about vague and unreal objectives such as human rights, the raising of living standards and democratization.* The day is not far off when we are going to have to deal in straight power concepts. The less we are hampered by idealistic slogans, the better." (Emphasis added)

(George Kennan: Head of Planning Staff, US State Department: 1948. Quoted in "War Against The Poor": Jack Nelson-Pallmeyer: Orbis Books, 1989)

Hasn't *this* been our actual creed? Wasn't this the game-plan which has formed us post-World War II? Isn't this what we *do*, no matter what we say?

But now ecology and even economy seem to be backing that oldtime religion. It seems we really do share one single blood after all: even the greed of the huge companies is beginning to face the fact that self-obliteration won't help profitability and to adjust itself to do some of the things they used to protest as 'unrealistic' and 'hopelessly uneconomic' (Recycling: removal of dangerous substances: energy efficiency). We even have the George Bushes and Margaret Thatchers suddenly discovering that, despite all the record: "I am an environmentalist" after all.

The 'global village' has been a commonplace among genuine environmentalists for years. It is the real small exquisite world speaking to us, pleading with us, not only for itself but for ourselves too. *For reality is our lifeblood: reality is us.* Each of us *does* affect the wellbeing of all the others: as they affect us. Just to survive we are at last beginning to see that we are mutually responsible, and therefore must learn mutual responsiveness. Not just "What have *they* done to the rain?": "What have *we* done...?": the helpless tears of Hiroshima and Glasgow and San Salvador.

We've known it all along. Maybe that's what the thin ghost of poor charity has been all this time: the spectre of all the murdered ones sitting down beside us at our table groaning with injustice. But because we haven't *behaved* as we claimed to believe, our whole society is traumatised. We are divided in our most secret selves, frightened to open the door. And so we close out our own future as well. The cancers of colonialism and neo-colonialism speak for themselves, every day more clamorously. The peoples of that Third World have had to endure them directly for centuries, but now these cancers are consuming themselves too: we, at the heart, are also in spasm, we can no longer "turn our heads, pretending we just don't see" (**Bob Dylan: Blowing In The Wind**). If any part of the one world is sick, we are sick.

I want to turn the page, there are marvellous things to write about, living here surrounded by such courage and such laughter.

They are what this song in high summer is all about.

But the running away has got to stop: that above all.

And this IS to turn the page. This is what the courage and the laughter give us.

Like Carlos and Susanna, we have to grow up. To take on the real world—all of it—and with it profound sorrow and genuine joy. We *have* to. The world is screaming at us there is no other option. We *have* to. To survive. Much more, to grow. To become ourselves. To laugh and think and live for ourselves once again. To escape the thralldom of the tinsel make believe of "Dallas" and Coca Cola, the soundbites, the laughter cards and the politicians, and to begin to believe again in ourselves and what we can do, are doing and are going to do, together. To take Victor's and Yanira's broken hands, with their priceless gifts of reality, of the one great dream:

"Levantate y mira la montaña:

Stand up and see: the wonder of the mountain

Source of the sun, the water and the wild wind
You who can harness the rush of mighty waters
You who, with the seed, sow the flight of your soul

Stand up and see: the hands with which you labour
Stretch out, join hands with this your neighbour
Growing together, with deepest blood united,
Knowing together the future *can be now."*

(Plegaria a un labrador: Prayer to a worker: Victor Jara)

There is no other way. Our present way is not working
after all—not for most of the people of the world. If we go
on as we are there will be no world for *all* the children, just
as there is already so little for most of the children. We can't
go on forever piling up the world's resources like Carlito
with his honey pot. The door is bulging inwards. Reality
refuses to be shut out forever. As the pollution mounds up,
we too will stifle. As the nuclear clouds spread, we too will
fall prey to radiation sickness. As the economically poorer
countries sink further into debt, our money too will
collapse. As we fund the murderers in Latin America, we
too lose the freedom for which we claim to be fighting. In
the end we can only keep out so much reality. And because
that reality is our life blood, the door *will* open: either
forced from without, with the terrible bloodbaths of catas-
trophe, or from within as we reach out to the rain and to
join our hands, receiving friendship.

There *are* signs of change: the beginnings of alternatives
to the chlorofluorocarbons; a smattering of arms control
agreements; the partial rejection of the contras.
But are they anything other than the drowning clutching
at straws? Are we now fooling ourselves into the ultimate
falsehood?:

"And, at the last, the greatest treason:
to do the right thing, for the wrong reason."

(T.S. Eliot: Murder in the Cathedral)

It's certainly too little so far. For longterm survival it may
very well be far too late: we may find that the world we have
laid waste so casually and so profoundly has just lain down
against the door to die, and, try desperately as we may, we
cannot now budge it.

The facts are large as life—and death.
Moron radio, pulp press and terminal television: the
tragic trio to which we have all but surrendered, are all
about keeping these facts—our lifeblood—from us. Our
culture has become a culture of pap, designed above all to
keep us "consuming."
Have you noticed how we have become "consumers"? All
our rich complexity shrunk to this little measure. At least
we used to be customers: 'The customer is always right'.
Whatever about that, the customer was at least one who
had to be 'customed': consulted about her requirements,
asked for his taste. Now our 'needs' are sold to us to suit the
products: we are fitted to the requirements of mass-
produced emphemera. To quote Jackson Browne:

"They sell us the President the same way
they sell us our clothes and our cars
They sell us everything from youth to religion
At the same time they sell us our wars—
Well, I want to know who the men in the shadows are
I want to hear somebody asking them why
We can count on them to tell us who our enemies are
But they're never the ones to fight or to die...?

And there are *lives* in the balance

There are people under fire
There are children at the cannon
And there is blood, blood on the wire..."

(Lives in the Balance)

We are indeed reduced to our littlest measure: we are allowed only to consume, not to question, or to interact, or genuinely to choose. And so we forcefeed ourselves food, insurance policies, cars, airplane seats and tickets, music, electricity, television programmes, holidays, coffins, bank loans...a strange diet indeed. In the end, like cancer, we consume one another and our imaginative, suffering, delighted selves. We are persuading ourselves that greed is OK: greed *is* reality, that's us. (This is my one problem with Jackson Browne's song: it isn't only forced on us from outside: *we* too are the "men in the shadows," because, in the end *we* are the ones who consume our appointed role as 'consumers.' And so we get the clothes, cars, religion, president/prime minister we (at least partly) deserve. And it's the other people who (mostly) get our wars, and have to give up their lives for our coffee.

The market planners and advertisers and weapons makers and politicians and musack manufacturers aren't from some other planet: they are us—who else? (We've even sold out our humour: compare Garfield the gluttonous cat of the 80s with Snoopy the philosophical dog of the 60s—and even Snoopy has become a T-shirt. If we can laugh at greed it *must* be alright, mustn't it?)

By contrast wht I love so much about the flamenco and the songs of revolution, Victor and Carlos Godoy, the Salvadorans and so many others, is that they dance even when the hard times come. And because of this, their sweetness is the more genuine, the richer. They "laugh all of their laughter, and weep all of their tears" indeed. They sing the silences of deep love, where joy and sorrow meet, where life and death come together.

And, above all, the thing we are not allowed is that precious silence.

For silence allows us to sing our *own* songs: silence breeds thought; silence echoes out the individual rhythms of each unique life; silence is stretching out in love, calling for response. Silence lets us laugh—laugh at our culture of unending clamour, where tragic news reports are punctured by trivial adverts, where everything is always 'Better!' or 'New!' or 'On Special Offer!' and where Death is always either on holiday, or the docile object of our voyeurism via The News or the latest "Make My Day" movie. And silence also allows us to mourn—healing our paralysing guilt, that last refuge of self-indulgence.

In that silence we can hear Victor's fingers snapping under the clubs; it catches the echo of the mother's silent tears, falling on her baby, sucking apathetically at her milkless breast; it is the stench from the opened mass grave, paid for with our dollars and pounds; it is the torturer's stick racking Yanira's womb...*And* it is the whisper of life, the still, small voice of hope, the echo of the music on the wind. "It is the faces and names and voices..."

We *must* grow up. "The war *is* real: the children *really* die: what *have* we done to the rain?"

For what is reality but another name for love?

And in reclaiming our right to that love, and with it our rights to mourn and to respond freely, to our sisters and brothers, with our own thought and laughter and not that programmed for us by the teleprompter, we also reclaim our own life and death and profound happiness.

And then, like all deep love, we can dare to open ourselves to the beauty within and beyond the pain: to listen, also, to the songs of lovely love; to hear, as well, the gentle stories around the campfires in the mountains beyond Esteli.

And to watch Yanira dance again.

"When you come back, my darling girl,
I know there will be shadows in your eyes
which I shall never be able to drive away;
I know there will be scars in your flesh
which I shall never be able to efface;
I know there will be censorship in your memory
which I shall never be able to lift;
I know there will be tremblings in your heart
which I shall never be able to calm;
And that there will be terrors in your soul
which I shall never be able to chase away.

But I promise you, my darling girl,
that I will weave spells
until the shadows are driven away;
I will wash your flesh
until the wounds are concealed;
I will search for oblivion
to calm your memory;
I will bring you sweet remembrances
until your mind is soothed;
And then I, on my knees,
bursting into a thousand flames
with the miracle of having you back,
will gather and heap up endearments,
as a nest where your spirit may shelter
from the explosion of that hell
you will have left far behind."

(Ely: a mother of the Plaza de Mayo, Argentina, speaking to her daughter, 'disappeared' by the military)

A poem for Ely's daughter, for Yanira, for Victor's Chile,
for the peoples of Argentina and Salvador, for the countries

themselves. For ourselves. As the Nicaraguans say: solidarity is the tenderness of the peoples.

The "greatest treason?" Is it really too late?
Who can say?
Certainly not me. For just as our partial civilisation can destroy the world totally, it also has the magnificent promise—once we have learned humility, and made friends with the world and its peoples—to transform the desert, while delighting in its silence. Wonderful things are happening. Suddenly, especially through their discovery of 'The Environment,' our politicians and economists and militarists are being shown up for what we have allowed them to be: seers blighted with tunnel vision, playing childish games with fire. Thanks to the blight, the bottle may be half empty now, but the clowns and jugglers and dancers are *choosing* that it's on the way to being full. All I know is: if Yanira can sing "My Own Revenge" then we *can* transform the world.

Perhaps it's just that we're learning to endure. One of the hallmarks of love is enduring on, no matter what. Maybe the greatest gift of recent times has been the fusing of poetry with anger and politics, giving us a wholeness which can carry us beyond ourselves to dream the dreams we never dared before, firing up our hearts: for my sister I would go to the ends of the earth. Friends give us back endurance. To transpose John's gospel: real love is irresistible because laying down our lives becomes the obvious and natural thing to do. Our lives for our friends. Our friends *are* our lives.

Endurance: weep when we have to, dance when we can. "If we can talk, we can sing; if we can walk, we can dance."

For there *are* two certain things. First that enduring love does work: the times are a-changing: increasingly rapidly. If they don't, if we won't change with them, there won't *be* any more times.

And second: we certainly *won't* be in time if we don't dare to dream and dance. There will be hundreds more Victors and Yaniras sent to the wall before we're through. As Yani says over and over: she's not so special; what she went through is routine in El Salvador, and usually they kill you too. And any of us can go out today and not come back: the war *is* real. *But* "the faces and names and voices of friends and people I'd known who had been tortured and killed came before my mind, and they had been so full of life, and now they were dead. I was only 22; I could not let their memory die, their work go for nothing; I had to go on living. They, those dear dead ones, gave me back my life." Loving endurance is her, their, gift to us.

In this most vital sense, it is never too late. Even if all the worst warnings came to awful fruit right now, and the whole world blew apart, Susanna would still just have settled on my lap in this last second, and Carlos would still just have fallen asleep on the couch beside us.

This, the loveliest thing, is clearest in these little guys: their simple, lovely, trust. Their absolute presence. One of the signs of hope at the present is how many friends in 'the movement' are having children: seizing the time with a vengeance. A few years back things were too grim, the dream too shrivelled, the future too dark. Maybe what we're realising is: whether we have a future and whatever about the past: we can choose *now*. We choose. *We* choose. We *choose*.

In Nunraw I read *East of Eden*. It moved me very much. Living here, just south of Steinbeck country, I've been reading it again. The whole book focuses on that choice: Cain and Abel, the choice for death or for life, smouldering in all of us. At the last, the story turns on the single Hebrew word: "Timshel": "Thou mayest": Choose: it's up to you. I wanted to quote it at length, but like the Native American who, civilized now, worships "before a painted landscape whose value is estimated in dollars", so Steinbeck, the defender of the little ones, has been subsumed into the system and is locked away behind prohibitive copyright fees. In essence he says: we are not programmed, not inescapably: through fear, apathy, guilt, greed, over-protective love, whatever. Whatever our circumstances, at the last Cain chooses to be Cain, Abel Abel. We choose, *we* choose, we *choose*. In the genuine real world, beyond the infantile jingles and the primitive lifestyles of Coke and McDonalds, waste and world leadership and superstardom, where 40 million people, countless other animals and species, and whole worlds of forest die each year directly through the workings of our present global economic/political system, the dispossessed are challenging us: "Why won't you join us? Why *do* you go on drinking and eating and throwing away without protest, without changing, when your food and drink and waste is grown in our blood and the blood of our children? In the destruction of all the world? Why *do* you allow your leaders to go on imposing *their* freedom on our peoples? Why? If you are not part of the solution, are you not part of the problem?"

There is no middle way: Edmund Burke has never made more sense:

"For the triumph of evil it is only necessary for good people to do nothing."

Or even just a little.

"We have assumed the names of peacemakers *but* we have been unwilling to pay any significant price for peace.
We want peace: *but* with half a heart, with half a life, half a will. The war continues because the waging of war is total but our waging of peace is partial."

(Daniel Berrigan)

To choose finally for life, for one world, one family over against all the odds: this is our wonder, this is our hope, this is the way to life. This is the challenge now: we know the facts, we can face them like adults and plan and slog and sing and endure and dance to help make the desert bloom. Or not.

"Think of the glory of the choice! A cat has no choice, a bee must make honey...'Thou mayest': this—this is a ladder to climb to the stars."

(East of Eden: John Steinbeck)

No matter where we are we can all find one more step to take. In friendship, to bring loving justice for all one step nearer. Take it. Now. And then another. There is no other way to real wealth, bursting life. We have to say to Valentina, to Victor, to Yanira:

"I *will* go with you: your people will be my people."

Against all the odds *they* chose, they *are choosing*. If they, after everything, can still sing 'Mi Venganza' and 'Nicaragua, Nicaraguita'—if, even yet, they can choose such life from the heart of all their anguish—so can we. 'The poor are always with us' because we so choose. By default, if not by design. By 'consuming' without question. We accept our coffee and the rest as part of that world order that sacrifices 40,000,000 human lives every year. Forty million human lives every year. Forty million lives every year. Immolated on mountains of trash, fired with the forests sacrificed for the nth billion hamburger, lit by the demonic children playing their games of greed and brutal power. Yanira, her people, the being-dispossessed, are choosing another way: This is not right, such a world order is obscene, insupportable, primitive: we are going to change it. Are you with us or not? Come on—it isn't as if it was even working!

And they are reaching out to us: Take these broken hands:

> "Stretch up, grow tall, hands joined with these your sisters
> Working together, by deepest blood united
> Knowing together the future *can be, now*."

And:

> "This guitar is not owned by the rich: how could it be?
> We sing of the scaffolding: set to reach up to the stars . . ."

Victor's stars, Steinbeck's stars. Nothing to do with escapism or other worlds or Hollywood's plastic dreams. These stars shine in our own hearts, we find them when every tree again becomes 'an object of reverence,' in the everyday steps of living less exploitatively, more creatively, constructing a peoples' politics, sharing all of our time, our money, our friendship, our lives: "laughing all our laughter, weeping all our tears . . ."

Today—wonderfully—Yanira got the worst of the splinters cut out. They had embedded inside her, and set up chronic infection. That's why the pain's been so bad for so long. (It still isn't enough. Her sisters were saying that, even now, two years after the attacks, her only chance of getting really well again is to rest up for months. And have a full operation. Fat chance! She is quite clear: the times are too critical for any of us to stop work. She is not special: too many have died, too many will have to die. She can't claim so much time for herself from the common pool—to say nothing of the $20,000 demanded for such treatment. And that's that. No heroics, no posturing: that's just the way it is.)

Well anyway, once more the odds are perhaps against massive surgery, for the time being. The doctor was even faintly hopeful that one day she may be able to carry a child again. Oh......

So the children have the last word. Little Carlos always gets me to sing him to sleep with his favourite song. I just did. He can't understand the thick Scots accent I'm sure (it's a shepherd singing tenderly to his pregnant lass)—but somehow...

It's desperately poignant that he loves *this* song so much, of course. But it's also magical in its tenderness, echoing the lovely hope and the enduring, irresistible song of all our Yaniras: "There are many orphans in El Salvador," she says. "Obviously you adopt them."

It's that "obviously" I love so much.

We will yet be able to sing Carlito's "Shearing" to his mother. One day:

"Oh the shearing's no' for you, my bonnie lassie-o
Ay, the shearing's no' for you, my bonnie lassie-o
The shearing's no' for you—for your back it willna bow
And your belly's rolling fu(ll), my bonnie lassie-o."

¡Ojala! Oh let it be.

¡Canta, Mi Pueblo, Canta!: Sing, Oh Sing, My People!

Song In High Summer is part of my work within *Echoes of Silence:* the music, and hopefully, some smattering of silence, in written form.

Taking as its keynote Nicaragua's "solidarity is the tenderness of the peoples," this network tries to echo the silences of grief and oppression, to amplify the whispers of resistance and the songs of lovely hope.

Echoes of Silence helps give voice to those whose voices are not heard within the world's structures of power. And to celebrate the lovely things that human beings go on accomplishing, even under extreme repression, whether of direct violence or the day-to-day grinding of material dispossession and impoverishment.

By focussing on this beauty, wherever it is to be found, we try to provide the loveliness and encouragement in endurance which building a genuinely just world requires, so helping the growth of one world people. A people whose first allegiance is to the children of *all* the earth, which is at home within all the lovely interdependencies of our tiny, fragile planet.

Echoes of Silence therefore works especially through community linking, informing, encouraging and organising, complementing the usual resources of booklets, films, videos, disussions, etc., with music, personal stories, and other live presentation. And always trying to offer concrete steps to take, projects to join, people to meet, things to be done.

It has the support of many individuals, community groups and organisations: El Salvador and Guatemala Human Rights Committee (UK); Chile Human Rights Committee (UK): Scottish Churches' Action for World

Development; Christian Aid; Sharing in Development Group; Chile Democratico (Scotland); CISPES (Committee in Solidarity with the People of El Salvador) (US); Nicaragua Network (US); Artists for the New Nicaragua; Artists for Peace through Justice; SCIAF; Office of the Americas; Cafe Victor Jara; OXFAM; and other justice and peace groups throughout Britain, Central America, the US and Canada.

While living within Leticia's branch of the one family, where the book has been written, I can also provide backup for the Salvadoran refugee community/justice organisations in their work; and help represent British and wider European opinion and feeling to Congress, other community leaders and the general public in the US. In addition I send news, analysis, music, interviews, recordings, etc. back to Britain (keying into the networks developed over the years with SEAD, OXFAM and the other agencies). And continue to serve as some small protection against renewed assault.

The 'green' guitar takes me all over, travelling in the US and in Europe, to give concerts, presentations, workshops, and to work with press, radio and television.

In all these ways information is shared, ideas are exchanged, connections made, and funds raised, especially for Yanira's work at the 'frontline' and to help pay the recurring costs of the medical treatment constantly necessary to cope with the worst effects of her brutal abuse.

Joan Rowley, a friend and longterm worker within the networks of peace through social justice, who was herself thrown into jail in El Salvador, has recently joined us. Working out of the Edinburgh office, she focuses especially on the British end of the work.

For more information/to book a concert/ presentation/ order more copies of *Song In High Summer*, etc., please

contact us at:

Echoes of Silence (USA): 686 South Arroyo Parkway, Suite 162, Pasadena, CA 91105, USA. (213) 257-1032.
    or
Echoes of Silence (UK): 41, George IV Bridge, Edinburgh EH1 1EL, SCOTLAND. (031) 225-1772.

All the proceeds from *Song In High Summer* are going to this work. If you, your community group and/or organisation, can make a donation of money and/or of time (promoting Yanira's work, setting up a concert or presentation, distributing this book), please do whatever you can—as soon as you can. Like the war being forced on her people, our support in resistance has to go on and on. For us it's cash, or time; for Yanira it's carrying her wounded self on from day to day, so that she can use her terrible experiences to help us understand what her people are suffering, so we can join them in their making justice, sharing with us their gentle, indomitable, endurance. As Victor would say, with his usual laughter:

"This thing is on its way: hang on tight—don't get left behind."

(Ni chicha, ni limona: Sitting on the Fence)

NATIONAL OFFICES

Britain

Amnesty International: 5, Roberts Place, Off Bowling Green, London EC1 0EJ

Campaign Against the Arms Trade: 11, Goodwin Street, Finsbury Park, London N4 3HQ

Campaign Coffee: 29, Nicolson Square, Edinburgh EH8 9BX

Campaign for Nuclear Disarmament: 22 - 24, Underwood Street, London N1 7GQ

Catholic Institute for International Relations: 22, Coleman Fields, London N1

Chile Solidarity Campaign: 20 - 21, Compton Terrace, London N1

Christian Aid: PO Box 100, London SE1 7RT and 41, George IV Bridge, Edinburgh EH1 1EL Scotland

El Salvador and Guatemala Human Rights Committees: 83, Margaret Street, London W1N 7HB

El Salvador Solidarity Campaign: 20 - 21, Compton Terrace, London N1

Friends of the Earth: 26 - 28, Underwood Street, London N1 7GQ

Nicaragua Solidarity Campaign: 20 - 21, Compton Terrace, London N1

OXFAM: 274, Banbury Road, Oxford and 36, Palmerston Place, Edinburgh, Scotland

Scottish Churches' Action for World Development: 41, George IV Bridge, Edinburgh EH1 1EL Scotland

Scottish Education and Action for Development: 29, Nicolson Square, Edinburgh EH8 9BX Scotland

Scottish Catholic International Aid Fund: 5, Oswald Street, Glasgow G1 4QR Scotland

Third World First: 232, Cowley Road, Oxford OX4 1UH

War on Want: Suite 4 - 6, The Hop Exchange, 24, Southwark Street, London SE 1

World Development Movement: Bedford Chambers, Covent Garden, London

USA

CISPES (Committee In Solidarity with the People of El Salvador): PO Box 12056, Washington DC 20005

Central America Resource Center: PO Box 2327, Austin, TX 78768

Christic Institute: 1324 North Capitol Street NW, Washington DC 20002

Coffee for Peace: PO Box 2435, Fort Bragg CA 95437

Committee for Health Rights in Central America: 513 Valencia Street, San Francisco CA 94110

DataCenter: 464 19th Street, Oakland CA 94612

EPOCA (Environmental Project on Central America): 13 Columbus Avenue, San Francisco CA 94111

FAIR (Fairness and Accuracy in Reporting): 666 Broadway, Suite 400, New York NY 10012

Food First/Institute for Food and Development Policy: 145 Ninth Street, San Francisco CA 94103

Honduras Information Center: 1 Summer Street, Somerville MA 02143

IFCO (Interreligious Foundation for Community Organization, Inc): 402 W. 145th Street, New York NY 10031

Interreligious Task Force on Central America: 475 Riverside Drive, Room 563, New York, NY 10115

MADRE Women's Peace Network: 121 West 27th Street, Room 301, New York NY 10001-6207

MASPS (Broad Movement of Support for the People of El Salvador): PO Box 292014, Los Angeles CA 90029

National Central America Health Rights Network: 853 Broadway, Room 416, New York NY 10003

National Lawyers Guild/Central American Task Force: 853 Broadway #1705, New York NY 10003

Nicaragua Network: 2025 I Street NW #212, Washington DC 20006

NISGUA (National Network in Solidarity with the People of Guatemala): 1314 14th Street NW, Washington DC 20005

NACLA (North American Congress on Latin America): 151 West 19th Street, New York NY 10011

Office of the Americas: 8124 West 3rd Street, Los Angeles CA 90048

OXFAM America: 115 Broadway, Boston MA 02116

Peace Development Fund: PO Box 270, Amherst MA 01004

Religious Task Force on Central America: 1747 Connecticut Avenue NW, Washington DC 20009

Somos Hermanas: 3543 18th Street, San Francisco CA 94110

Trade for Peace, Inc.: PO Box 3190, Madison WI 53704-0190

Ventana (Artists/cultural workers against US intervention): 339 Lafayette Street, New York NY 10012

Veterans Peace Action Team: PO Box 586, Santa Cruz CA 95061

Voices on the Border: PO Box 53081 Temple Heights Station, Washington DC 20009

Washington Office on Latin America: 110 Maryland Avenue NE, Washington DC 20002

Witness for Peace: PO Box 29497, Washington DC 20017